Total Marketing

The business of integrating consumers, employees, and company networks

Mara Cassinari
and
Frank Pagano

Series in Business and Finance

VERNON PRESS

www.vernonpress.com

In the Americas:	*In the rest of the world:*
Vernon Press	Vernon Press
1000 N West Street, Suite 1200,	C/Sancti Espiritu 17,
Wilmington, Delaware 19801	Malaga, 29006
United States	Spain

Series in Business and Finance

Library of Congress Control Number: 2025944337

ISBN: 979-8-8819-0392-3

Also available: 979-8-8819-0349-7 [Hardback]; 979-8-8819-0390-9 [PDF, E-Book]

Contents

List of Acronyms

4 P-s	Product, Price, Placement, Promotion
ABB	Asea Brown Boveri
AI	Artificial Intelligence
AR	Augmented Reality
B2B	Business To Business
B2B2C	Business To Business To Consumer
B2C	Business To Consumer
BBC	British Broadcasting Corporation
BoA	Bank of America
Capex	Capital Expenditures
CBDC	Central Bank Digital Currency
CDP	Customer Data Platform
CEO	Chief Executive Officer
CFO	Chief Financial Officer
CHRO	Chief Human Resources Officer
CIO	Chief Information Officer
CLV	Customer Lifetime Value
CMO	Chief Marketing Officer
COGS	Cost Of Goods Sold
CPM	Cost Per Thousand
CRM	Customer Relationship Management
CRO	Contract Research Organization
CSAT	Customer Satisfaction *(Score)*
CTO	Chief Technology Officer
CX	Customer Experience
CXO	Chief Experience Officer
DAO	Decentralized Autonomous Organization
DeFi	Decentralized Finance
DPP	Digital Product Passport
DTC	Direct To Consumer
EBITDA	Earnings Before Interest, Taxes, Depreciation, Amortization
ETF	Exchange Traded Fund
EU	European Union
EX	Employee Experience
FDA	Food and Drug Administration
FMCG	Fast Moving Consumer Goods
FTE	Full Time Employee
GA	Google Analytics
GDPR	General Data Protection Regulation
Gen AI	Generative Artificial Intelligence
HR	Human Resources
ID	Identity
IoB	Internet of Behavior
IoT	Internet of Things
IT	Information Technology

KPI	Key Performance Indicator
LLM	Large Language Model
MAU	Monthly Average Users
MIT	Massachusetts Institute of Technology
MR	Mixed Reality
MX	Multiexperience
NFT	Non-Fungible Token
NPS	Net Promoter Score
OEM	Original Equipment Manufacturer
P&L	Profit and Loss *(Account)*
PYUSD	PayPal's stablecoin (anchored to the US dollar)
R&D	Research and Development
RPA	Robotic Process Automation
RWA	Real World Assets
RWD	Real World Data
SME	Small Medium Enterprise
SMS	Short Message Service
STEM	Science, Technology, Engineering and Mathematics
TCNA	Toyota Connected North America
TM	Total Marketing
TX	Total Experience
USDC	Circle's stablecoin (anchored to the US dollar)
USDT	Tether's stablecoin (anchored to the US dollar)
USZ	Universitätsspital Zürich
UX	User Experience
VIP	Very Important Person
VR	Virtual Reality
WEF	World Economic Forum
ZKP	Zero Knowledge Proof

Featuring:

Exclusive interview with Daron Acemoglu, 2024 Economics Nobel Prize winner

Contributors:

Marco Di Dio Roccazzella, Cecilia Marchi, Massimo Morini, Giuseppe Stigliano, Roberta Virtuani

Foreword 1

Marco Di Dio Roccazzella[1]

We live in an era where the boundaries between physical and digital, between real and virtual, are dissolving at a dizzying pace. Every interaction, every touchpoint, every connection carries with it a fragment of a broader, more complex, and integrated experience. At the heart of this new paradigm stands the concept of Total Experience (TX[2]), an approach Gartner has aptly defined as the synergistic union of four fundamental elements: Customer Experience (CX), Employee Experience (EX), User Experience (UX), and Multiexperience (MX). But what does it really mean to live this totality of experiences?

Technology, once merely a tool, has now become a bridge connecting worlds and dimensions. TX invites us to rethink not only how companies interact with customers but also how these customers, along with employees, users, and ecosystems, participate in a global experience. It is not just a sum of individual experiences; it is a true symphony in which every note, every silence, every harmony contributes to creating a whole, which is greater than the sum of its parts.

For many years, as we leafed through marketing manuals and management texts, we read about one-to-one marketing as a revolutionary promise, an ideal future where every company could interact with each customer in a unique and personalized way. Yet, this promise remained, for a long time, a chimera, or an unfulfilled expectation. The reality of mass marketing often took precedence, with standardized approaches, insensitive to individual needs and preferences.

Today, however, the advent of exponential technologies, like artificial intelligence (AI), is turning that promise into reality. Thanks to AI, indeed, companies can now analyze vast amounts of data in real-time, understand customers' behaviors, desires, and emotions, and offer truly personalized

---

[1] General Manager, Jakala.

[2] We will describe in full depth the idea of TX in our Chapter 1. The TX model was created in 2022. For more information, see: https://webinar.gartner.com/445952/agenda/session/1051272?login=ML. The Total Experience model is also a key pillar of the 2024 Gartner Hype Cycle for Emerging Technologies; for more info, see: https://www.gartner.com/en/newsroom/press-releases/2024-08-21-gartner-2024-hype-cycle-for-emerging-technologies-highlights-developer-productivity-total-experience-ai-and-security. GARTNER and HYPE CYCLE are trademarks of Gartner, Inc. and/or its affiliates.

experiences. The dream of one-to-one marketing is materializing, not just as a market strategy but as a key element of what we define as Total Marketing. Technology is not merely a driver of automation but a facilitator of authentic and meaningful connections, capable of bridging the gap between theoretical ideals and daily practice.

However, with this power comes significant ethical issues. The use of personal data, the ability to collect, analyze, and utilize someone else's information to create personalized experiences, raises fundamental questions about privacy, consent, and fairness. Technology, while offering extraordinary opportunities, brings with it the responsibility to ensure that data is handled with the utmost respect and transparency. It is imperative that companies do not view data merely as a resource to exploit but as a shared asset with their consumers, who should be fully aware of how information is used and value is generated from it.

In this context, a new ethics of value-sharing emerges. It is not enough to collect data to improve services or increase sales. It is necessary to return some of that value to consumers, in terms of enhanced experiences, but also through deeper and more transparent engagement. Companies must strive to create a fair balance where the benefits generated from the use of data are shared, establishing a relationship of mutual trust. This approach could lead to the definition of new key performance indicators (KPIs) that go beyond traditional metrics and measure aspects such as trust, transparency, and customer perception of value. Moreover, value-sharing could stimulate the development of new economic and business models, where collaboration with the consumer becomes central and where co-creation of value underpins future business strategies.

What is Total Marketing, in a nutshell? If we pause for a moment to reflect, we realize that Total Marketing is, in its essence, an extension of an ancient truth: Human experience has never been linear or monochromatic. Our lives have always been woven from a complex tapestry of relationships, perceptions, emotions, and interactions that, when viewed from a broader perspective, reveal a rich and intricate design. The concept of totality, in its deepest sense, invites us to see every fragment of reality as part of a greater whole. As the Greek philosopher Heraclitus reminded us, that everything flows and that everything is in constant interaction with the rest, Total Experience pushes us to think not just about individual moments but about the continuous flow that unites experiences and people.

This book aims to explore the vast territory of Total Marketing, not only as a strategic model for the future of organizations but also as a philosophy for interpreting and shaping our contemporary world. As a lens through which we can grasp the complexity of the human and technological dynamics that shape our daily lives. In the journey that follows, we will delve into the challenges and opportunities that it offers. We will discover how companies can leverage this holistic approach to enhance customer and employee engagement, making the experience a unified expression of value and meaning. But above all, we will reflect on how this vision can enrich our understanding of the world and our place in it.

In the end, perhaps, we will understand that Total Marketing is not just about what we see or touch. It is a journey that invites us to explore how we perceive, understand, and connect with others, with the deep desire to create experiences that are not only functional but also meaningful, authentic, and, above all, just.

Total Marketing is the product of a vision that transcends traditional logic to embrace a world of infinite possibilities, where technology, ethics, and creativity merge to shape the future.

Foreword 2

Roberta Virtuani[1]

In the rapidly changing world of digital transformation, Total Marketing offers a forward-thinking approach for businesses aiming to deepen their engagement with customers, employees, and partners. Authored by Mara Cassinari and Frank Pagano, this book explores the intersection of marketing, technology, and organizational strategy, providing practical frameworks that help organizations navigate complex challenges while staying aligned with modern expectations.

This approach is particularly valuable for its step-by-step guidance, enabling businesses to align their marketing practices with the evolving demands of today's stakeholders. The book equips readers with tools to evaluate and refine their strategies, integrating cutting-edge technologies like artificial intelligence (AI) and blockchain to create personalized experiences that resonate across diverse audiences. AI serves as a transformative force, allowing companies to anticipate customer needs, optimize resources, and craft hyper-personalized journeys that enhance engagement and drive loyalty.

As Andrew Ng, a pioneer in the AI field, aptly puts it, "AI is the new electricity. Just as electricity transformed industry after industry 100 years ago, I think AI will now do the same."[2] Total Marketing demonstrates how organizations can harness this new "energy" to redefine the marketing experience. Blockchain further enhances this transformation by providing secure, transparent frameworks that increase trust and accountability in customer interactions, fostering stronger, more transparent relationships. Together, AI and blockchain empower organizations to not only improve efficiency but also to establish meaningful, responsible connections with modern audiences.

Over time, marketing has evolved from a one-dimensional transaction into a complex web of experiences, interactions, and relationships. What was once a linear exchange has transformed into a dynamic ecosystem, where every

---

[1] Roberta Virtuani is Senior Assistant Professor and Research Fellow of Organizational Theory and Design and Personal Development at Università Cattolica del Sacro Cuore.

[2] On January 25, 2017, Andrew Ng—co-founder of Google Brain, Coursera co-founder, and founder of the AI Fund and DeepLearning.AI—spoke at the Stanford MSx Future Forum. During his talk, he discussed how artificial intelligence is transforming the industries, showcasing the opportunities and its impact on the society. The video is available at: https://www.youtube.com/watch?v=21EiKfQYZXc.

touchpoint—whether customer, employee, or partner—adds new layers of meaning and value. In this context, the book emerges as a comprehensive answer to the fragmented experiences often found in today's digital world. Rather than isolating Customer Experience (CX) from Employee Experience (EX), or viewing Multiexperience (MX) as separate from User Experience (UX), the framework weaves them together, aiming for cohesion in a world that is constantly on the verge of change.

This volume also stands out for its rich collection of case studies and expert interviews. These examples illustrate how industry leaders adapt their strategies to stay competitive, streamline operations, and cultivate a culture of continuous improvement. By showcasing how these companies leverage AI and blockchain, the volume provides actionable insights into the essential steps for building deeper connections and innovating in today's fast-paced market. Each case offers a practical example, highlighting how exponential technologies can drive both operational efficiency and transformative customer engagement.

Beyond technological and operational advancements, Total Marketing champions ethical considerations as foundational to modern marketing. In a world where data has become the currency of interaction, there is an undeniable responsibility to handle it with care and integrity. The authors emphasize transparency, trust, and fair value-sharing between companies and their communities. As organizations increasingly adopt technologies like AI and blockchain, prioritizing ethical standards becomes critical. By fostering transparency and accountability, the book underscores how responsible practices can underpin strategies that are both effective and aligned with principles of fairness, trust, and loyalty.

Total Marketing serves as an essential resource for leaders and marketers seeking to drive digital transformation and innovation. Combining strategic insights with real-world applications, it provides a roadmap for building stronger, more meaningful connections with all stakeholders in a digital-first world. Whether readers are assessing current strategies or exploring the latest in exponential technologies, this book offers the guidance and inspiration needed to succeed in an ever-evolving landscape.

Ultimately, this work invites readers to look beyond immediate business outcomes and consider the broader impact of their work on society. It is not only about seeing what is but about envisioning what could be—a world where technology, ethics, and imagination unite to shape a future that values connection, transparency, and authenticity. This journey through Total Marketing is both a roadmap and a reflection on how we understand and create experiences that are not only functional but also meaningful, authentic, and, above all, fair.

Introduction: If Only We Knew

Mara Cassinari

Frank Pagano

Between 2016 and 2020, the Department of Cardiac Surgery at the University Hospital of Zurich, Switzerland (called USZ, Universitätsspital Zürich), registered a sudden increase in death cases, reaching a level that was deemed as very unusual, if compared to the Swiss and international averages. Nobody noticed, not even the C-Room of the hospital, until a local media publication, in May 2020[1] (in the middle of the first COVID-19 crisis), raised suspicions against the head of the department (he left USZ in 2021, "consensually," as the official note to the press read). The accusations pointed at the use of heart implants, which were developed by a company co-owned by the surgeon[2]. It turned out that the testing protocols of the devices had been embellished to accelerate the approval for experimentation on humans.

Even though the case dates to a few years ago, in 2024 the management of the hospital called for a thorough investigation on the matter, as the defective devices might have an impact overtime, also on patients who did not suffer lethal complications, therefore potentially causing a long tail of deaths and the risk of a class action suit against the medical institution. In all cases, the CEO of USZ said that "we cannot let the past rest," meaning that there is an ethical obligation for whatever healthcare organization to own the truth, and to understand what went wrong in the process that led to what the successor of the head surgeon defined a "disaster" and "criminal and unethical behavior."

This is, for sure, a rare case. Mistakes of this magnitude and frauds are not common, fortunately. Regardless, should we track what we do, as public and private entities, from supply chain to the delivery of final experiences, so that it doesn't take eight years to launch a task force to reconcile events and responsibilities? Can technology help us to extract, at scale and virtually no cost, some social value and shared truth from relevant data of users, employees and suppliers, without violating industrial secrets and everyone's privacy? Can exponential technologies, especially, make sense of massive amounts of facts,

---

[1] The publication, belonging to the Swiss media company Tamedia, is called Tages Anzeiger - www.tagesanzeiger.ch.

[2] We will not mention any name, as we are interested in the case per se, and especially in the asymmetry of information in a strategic industry, like healthcare.

to enable us to craft better and more personalized experiences and progressively more effective innovations? Shouldn't there be an interest in leaving a trace of the content and the process of our operations, so that we minimize noise, the temptation to fool the system, and time to justice? If only we had the data, we might think. If only we knew.

This doesn't apply only to strategic industries, like healthcare, real estate, mobility, education and energy, which account for most of family budgets. This is also useful for any consumer experience. Should data, once refined and anonymized, or treated according to national and regional laws, have social relevance and visibility in case of controversies? Should data be captured, monetized, and used to unlock the full value of what we do as humans in our communities and economies, for all parties involved? Marketing has always been a game of prioritizing users' satisfaction, while delivering a profit to shareholders, with side effects outsourced to the broader community or to governments. Employees and suppliers are important, but very often perceived as fungible by shareholders and boardrooms, especially when times are tough.

What does marketing look like when we introduce the idea of making sense of the world around us, and serving the right information to the right people, at the right time, while fairly compensating all actors of the network around us? We are not referring here to transparent supply chains and equitable policies in hiring suppliers or employees, driven by purpose. Sure, my salad dressing mix or my T-shirt should be manufactured without anyone having to see their rights violated or disrespected. There is more to this than purpose. Moreover, we are not questioning capitalism or its essence. We are so pro-market that we believe there should be a market for data and digital 'work.' Total Marketing elevates, as a matter of fact, capitalism to a new level. Total Marketing doesn't want to replace existing marketing theories, but stresses one simple truth: the enormous power contained in everyone's agency and data, and how those could be placed at the service of all players in whatever value chain.

Exponential technologies are giving superpowers to humans and data, unlocking tremendous value, with major efficiencies to be gained while running the planet. In today's digital age, to use the marketing jargon, creating connections that are seamless, efficient, and technology-driven is not just an advantage; it's a necessity for businesses of all sizes, public and private.

What we are going to do in this book is to describe the advent of what we call Total Marketing, namely a comprehensive and holistic approach that brings together all stakeholders into a cohesive and interconnected ecosystem, powered by tech. Today's marketing needs experiences that are heavily imbued with technology. To use Gartner's terminology, it needs a Total Experience as its foundation[3].

Total Marketing is created by an ever-changing layer of exponential technologies, among which AI, of course, and blockchains, and by the need for a culture change across the whole web of consumers, employees and suppliers. The truth is, we are all linked, and our goal should be to increase social capital for everyone and reach service excellence, with minimum impact on the outer community, and zero noise, asymmetries, and negative externalities.

Total Marketing means that our input, whoever we are in the food chain, is captured via a hybrid net of phygital interfaces and devices, and processed instantly and intelligently, with the final output being the result of the perfect allocation and use of available resources, served to anyone in a fair and ultra-personalized fashion, measured exactly against their needs and desires, present and future. There will be no other way to do business in the future. All stakeholders will have, thanks to technology, the incentives and the tools to co-create a shared future. The main finding of this work is that this vision is technologically feasible. It's up to us to decide how badly we want a transparent, efficient and effective economy, where everyone wins. It's up to us to shape new standards and values for Total Marketing to bring about its benefits to the entire network of fans, brand owners and suppliers.

The benefits of technology and automation are massive. What about us, the humans? What will we do when technology frees us from the most boring and bureaucratic chores and rituals of our existence? We'll rethink the way we produce, track, own our data and agency, physically and digitally, so that we can build better strategic industries and more engaging branded experiences, calibrated *ad personam*, transparent and secure, fully unfolding our social rights and responsibilities, on top of the satisfaction of our individual utility.

The good news is that we are finally able to measure the world and estimate our social worth, besides the mere exercise of pleasing our personal spending instincts. We can calculate the social impact of our being here. Traditional Marketing was about 'me,' my personal utility as a fan and its value for my

---

[3] Total Experience is a concept and framework by research institution Gartner. For more information, see https://webinar.gartner.com/445952/agenda/session/1051272?login=ML. Total Marketing refers to how the marketing mix changes considering exponential technologies, like AI and Blockchain, and of the Total Experience that unfolds thanks to them. Total Marketing is all stakeholders' satisfaction, at a fair profit for all. Total Marketing, we will see, is taking responsibility for the full network revolving around a company or an organization, engaging all players, to deliver extraordinary experiences, which are beneficial for the one and the many at the same time, let alone the environment.

favorite brand or service provider (the so-called Customer Lifetime Value, or CLV). Total Marketing[4] is the measure of the interaction of the broader us. We did not have the data, and even if we had the data, we were not able to make sense of it. Until today.

We are all connected, and, to paraphrase the new head surgeon at USZ in Zurich, we cannot let the future rest. Now we know, and we can. Do we want to?

---

[4] The idea of a 'Total Marketing' has been generated and crafted by the two authors, Mara Cassinari and Frank Pagano. Chapter 5 of this volume is co-written with Cecilia Marchi and Marco Di Dio Roccazzella (he also wrote the Foreword), who are external contributors to the book.

Chapter One
The Pillars of the Total Experience

Mara Cassinari

In a rapidly evolving and hyper-connected business landscape, organizations face the dual challenge of attracting and retaining both customers and employees. This has led to the emergence of the Total Experience (TX) strategy, a comprehensive approach that integrates multiple disciplines, creating a seamless and superior ecosystem for all stakeholders.

Total Experience (TX), introduced by Gartner as one of the top technology trends for 2021, brings together four key experience areas: Customer Experience (CX), Employee Experience (EX), User Experience (UX), and Multiexperience (MX). By combining these disciplines, TX creates a unified and enhanced overall experience that benefits everyone involved in an organization.[1]

The core objective of Total Experience is to break down the silos between these areas, ensuring a seamless collaboration that aligns with any organization's broader goals. This comprehensive strategy not only enhances each individual experience but also offers a competitive advantage by delivering a superior, interconnected experience, which aligns with the needs and expectations of both clients and staff.

Total Experience gained relevance during the COVID-19 pandemic, where interactions increasingly shifted to mobile, virtual, and distributed formats. By focusing on TX, organizations can better adapt to these new realities, meeting the higher expectations of today's digital-first customers, and maintain employee satisfaction and productivity in a more distributed work environment.

This framework leverages technology to enable seamless interactions across various touchpoints and platforms, allowing businesses to respond flexibly and quickly to the evolving needs of their stakeholders. Additionally, it focuses on using insights from these interactions to keep improving and innovating its services and products.

---

[1] Gartner, Top Strategic Technology Trends for 2021, Brian Burke. GARTNER is a trademark of Gartner Inc. and/or its affiliates. This Gartner report is archived and is included for historical context only.

1.1 The Components of the Total Experience

Customer Experience, Employee Experience, User Experience, and Multiexperience play a unique role in shaping how people interact with and feel about a company or a brand.

Figure 1.1: Total Experience, a holistic approach[2].

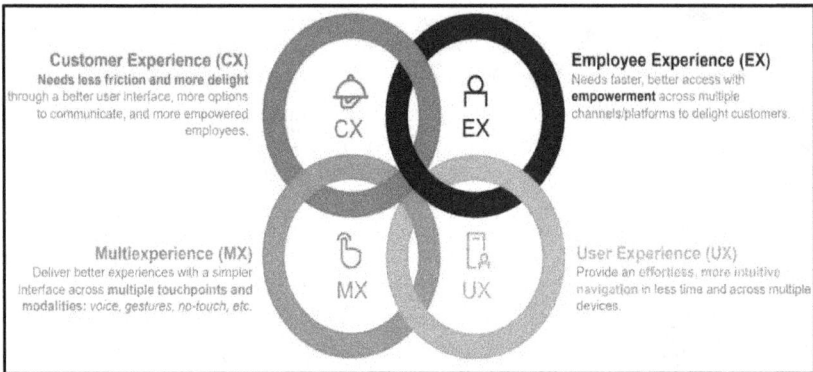

Customer Experience: Think of CX as the sum of every interaction a customer has with a company, from browsing the website to getting help from customer support. It's the overall impression they walk away with, influencing their loyalty and how they view your brand.

Employee Experience: This is all about the journey your employees take with a company, from their first day on the job to their last. EX covers their work environment, the tools provided, and their overall engagement with the workplace. A positive EX means a more engaged and productive workforce.

User Experience: UX pays close attention to how users interact with products and services. It's about making sure its interactions are as enjoyable and efficient as possible, increasing satisfaction and encouraging them to return.

Multiexperience: In an increasingly interconnected environment, MX focuses on creating a seamless experience across various platforms and devices. Whether it's a mobile app, a web interface, or even wearable tech, MX ensures that every interaction feels connected and easy to use.

---

[2] Michelle Duerst, Don Scheibenreif, *The Total Experience Strategy for Better Retail Digital Interactions*, Gartner, July 29, 2021. Available at: https://webinar.gartner.com/445952/agenda/session/1051272?login=ML. This Gartner content is archived and is included for historical context only.

As we go through each of these areas, we'll uncover how they all work together to build a holistic and successful strategy for your organization.

1.1.1. Customer Experience

Customer Experience is the internal and subjective response customers have to both direct and indirect contacts with a company. Unlike isolated interactions, CX represents a holistic perception, which is developed over time, influenced by a company's integrated efforts across all departments during the following key phases:

Understanding customers and defining personas

At the heart of the CX strategy is a deep understanding of your customers. This goes beyond simple demographics or purchasing habits; it's about knowing what drives them, what challenges they face, and what brings them joy. To do this, we create detailed personas based on real data from surveys, interviews, and behavioral insights. These personas then inform every decision, ensuring that products and services are designed with the customer in mind.

Defining customer expectations, setting goals, and positioning

Knowing our customers allows us to set clear expectations and align our business capabilities with customer expectations of our brand. This alignment manifests itself as a brand promise that resonates with our market positioning and the distinct value we offer. Clear expectations provide a benchmark for measuring all customer interactions, thereby building trust and reinforcing our brand's reputation.

Journey mapping your customer personas

Journey mapping turns personas into visual stories of how customers interact with your brand, from discovering your products to becoming loyal advocates. This process helps you spot key "moments of truth" where customers make decisions, as well as chances to surprise and delight them. Tailoring these journeys to different customer segments allows you to create more engaging and personalized experiences that boost loyalty.

Measure the experience

To truly understand CX, we don't just measure overall satisfaction or individual interactions; we focus on the entire journey. By tracking satisfaction at every stage, we can pinpoint exactly where customers are happy or frustrated. Using advanced technologies, we gather real-time feedback from multiple channels, allowing us to continuously assess and quickly address any issues. This detailed approach ensures we are always adapting to meet evolving customer expectations and market demands.

Analyze the experience

The data we collect gives us valuable insights into the Customer Experience. By reviewing feedback and tracking metrics, we can spot patterns and trends that help shape our strategies. This analysis shows why certain experiences stand out, helping us improve and better meet customer expectations along their journey.

Improve the experience

The insights we gain from this analysis help us make improvements to the Customer Experience. Whether it's fixing a frustrating process or enhancing a feature customers love, every change is part of an ongoing feedback loop. This constant cycle of learning and refining ensures our CX strategy stays aligned with customer needs and continues to exceed expectations.

1.1.2. Employee Experience

Employee Experience is an essential component of the broader Total Experience framework. It specifically focuses on the journey an employee takes within a company, from recruitment to retirement, and is shaped by the company's culture, the physical and digital environments provided, the tools and technology available, and the interpersonal relationships fostered within the workplace.

Adapting to change with flexible work arrangements

The COVID-19 pandemic has reshaped traditional workspaces, prompting a shift toward more adaptable work conditions. Organizations now recognize the necessity of flexible work arrangements such as remote working, hybrid models, and variable hours to support diverse employee needs and lifestyles. This flexibility not only reinforces employee well-being but also equips companies to handle future disruptions more effectively.

Enhanced digital tools and automation

Investing in superior digital tools for communication and collaboration has become an imperative in the wake of widespread remote and hybrid work models. Beyond basic tools, the introduction of automation and AI-driven technologies like copilots can revolutionize workflows. These technologies automate routine tasks, enabling employees to focus on more complex and creative tasks, which enhances productivity and job satisfaction. Continuous training in these new tools ensures employees are equipped to adapt and excel in an evolving work environment.

Employee well-being and support

In today's fast-paced, high-stress environments, ensuring the well-being of employees has become more crucial than ever. Companies must offer resources to manage stress, foster mental resilience, and promote holistic health. This can include wellness programs, mental health days, and supportive HR policies that help employees cope with the unique challenges they face.

Continuous learning and AI integration

As technology evolves, so do job roles. Offering continuous learning, especially in areas like AI and automation, is crucial. This not only enhances employees' skills but also keeps them engaged and motivated, ready to embrace and lead technological changes.

Employee feedback and participation

It's important for companies to have regular feedback systems that give employees a chance to share their experiences and suggest improvements. By using this data strategically, companies can better align their operations with the needs of employees and market demands, improving both the EX and the TX.

Unified data analytics

Using analytics brings together information from different points in both employee and customer journeys. This gives insights into behavior, preferences, and pain points. This strategic use of data analytics aligns operational practices with employee needs and market demands, enhancing both EX and TX.

Cultural and leadership commitment

A strong commitment from leadership is essential for creating a positive Employee Experience. Leaders should model values of empathy, transparency, and responsiveness. By aligning the company's goals with the well-being of both employees and customers, leaders can foster a culture where everyone thrives.

Inclusive and diverse work environment

Building an inclusive culture that respects and values diversity improves the Employee Experience. It creates a sense of belonging, encourages innovation, and helps employees connect with customers in more empathetic ways. This boosts both business performance and customer relationships.

1.1.3. User Experience

UX is about designing products, services, events, and journeys, keeping the user's needs in mind. It focuses on understanding users, what they need, what they value, their abilities, and their limitations, while also considering their business goals. The objective is to create experiences that are enjoyable, efficient and aligned with what users expect at every touchpoint. Some key areas to enhance UX are:

Consistency across channels

Make sure that User Experience is consistent across all platforms. Whether a customer interacts with your service online, through a mobile app, or in-store, the experience should feel seamless and cohesive.

Accessibility and inclusivity

Design for accessibility to ensure all users, including those with disabilities, can enjoy a positive User Experience. Inclusivity means thinking about the full range of human diversity, such as language, culture, gender, ability, and age.

Personalization

Use data analytics to understand user needs and preferences. Offering personalized experiences can make interactions feel more relevant and tailored to each user.

Feedback mechanisms

Add automated feedback systems to your digital platforms to collect insights at key touchpoints, like after a purchase, interaction. These systems help to gather real-time feedback and make design improvements more effectively.

Performance and speed

In the digital world, the speed and efficiency of website and app interfaces can greatly impact UX. Make sure that digital platforms perform well on different devices and network connections.

Emotional engagement

Create experiences that connect with users emotionally. This can be done through storytelling, great design, and interactive elements that resonate on a deeper level.

Continuous testing and optimization

UX is always evolving, and it's important to keep it improving based on user feedback and behavior. Regular testing, including A/B testing and usability studies, helps you ensure the experience is aligned with user expectations and keeps up with technology.

1.1.4. Multiexperience

Multiexperience is about creating seamless interactions across different devices and ways of interacting, like touch, voice, and gestures. It goes beyond just having a consistent user interface across different platforms; it's about integrating a wide range of interaction types into the overall User Experience with a brand or technology.[3]

For instance, augmented and virtual reality are changing how we engage with the digital world. We're moving away from traditional screens and keyboards, towards more immersive and intuitive interfaces, like conversational interfaces and gesture controls. MX transforms the delivery of technology by:

Enhancing modalities

MX designs for various ways of interacting, whether it's traditional methods like keyboards or newer ones like touch, voice, gestures, and augmented reality. This flexibility allows users to engage with services in the most natural way, depending on their context, like using a voice assistant while driving or a touch interface on the go.

Embracing device diversity

Multiexperience recognizes the wide range of devices users rely on, from smartphones and tablets to wearables and immersive technology. Each type of device brings unique opportunities for interaction, and when these are seamlessly integrated, they enhance the User Experience.

Ensuring app consistency

Applications should maintain visual and functional consistency across devices. This means users can smoothly switch from one device to another, like starting a task on a desktop and finishing it on a smartphone, without any disruption.

Integrating interaction types

Multiexperience seamlessly blends different interaction methods. A user might start a task with a voice command, continue it with touch, or use augmented reality to try a product, before purchasing it through an app.

Contextualizing the User Experience

MX also considers the user's context, such as location, time of day, or type of device. This real-time understanding helps deliver more relevant and personalized experiences.

Achieving coherence and consistency

A key part of MX is ensuring that no matter what device or platform users engage with, the experience remains consistent and high-quality. Whether they

---

[3] For more information on the definition of Multiexperience, please refer to Gartner's official glossary: https://www.gartner.com/en/information-technology/glossary/multi experience-development-platforms-mxdp.

are using a smartphone, laptop, or other device, the experience should feel familiar and smooth.

To achieve this, it's important to create a unified brand experience with consistent design elements like logos, colors, and overall aesthetics. This reinforces brand identity and builds trust.

1.2. Weaving experiences into a unified strategy

The integration of Customer Experience, Employee Experience, User Experience, and Multiexperience into a Total Experience strategy embodies a strategic transformation in organizational culture and operations. Adopting a TX approach is no longer just a trend; it's becoming essential for businesses looking to stay competitive.

According to a 2021 report by Gartner, by 2026, 60% of large enterprises will have transformed their business model through Total Experience, resulting in top-class customer and employee levels.[4]

CX and EX: A symbiotic relationship

Customer Experience and Employee Experience are closely connected. Happy and engaged employees are more likely to provide better customer service, which leads to higher customer satisfaction and loyalty. For instance, a Gallup study found that companies with highly engaged employees see a 10% boost in customer ratings and a 20% increase in sales.[5] By creating an EX environment that focuses on empowerment, recognition, and support, businesses can enhance both employee morale and Customer Experience.

UX and MX: Crafting seamless engagements

User Experience plays a key role in shaping Multiexperience. MX is designed to ensure consistent and streamlined interactions across various touchpoints and modalities, including web, mobile, wearable devices, and conversational interfaces.

Emerging Technologies like AI and chatbots are simplifying these seamless engagements. According to McKinsey[6] companies that implement personalized

---

[4] Gartner, 2021. "Top Strategic Technology Trends for 2022. 12 Trends Shaping the Future of Digital Business." This Gartner report is archived and is included for historical context only.

[5] *State of American Workplace*, Gallup, 2017. This finding is based on a meta-analysis of 339 studies conducted across 230 organizations in 49 industries and 73 countries. The research involved more than 82,000 businesses and over 1.8 million employees, to calculate the relationship between employee engagement and business performance outcomes, including customer loyalty, profitability and productivity.

[6] Avinash Chandra Das et al., *The next frontier of customer engagement: AI-enabled customer service*, McKinsey & Company, 2023.

and digitally enabled solutions can resolve over 95% of service interactions through digital channels like chatbots and self-service tools.

Integrating UX principles is essential for crafting intuitive and engaging interfaces that help users navigate across platforms without friction.

EX enhancing UX

According to the Microsoft 2017 Global Customer Service Report, 72% of customers expect agents to know their contact history and previous engagements, underlining the need for seamless experiences.[7]

The experience of employees can directly influence the design and implementation of user interfaces and services. When employees have a positive experience and have access to the latest tools and technologies, they are more likely to innovate in their work. Integrating UX principles is essential to crafting intuitive and engaging interfaces that help both agents and users navigate across platforms without friction.

This innovation can lead to the development of more user-centric designs and functionalities, thereby enhancing UX. Furthermore, when organizations foster a culture of collaboration among developers, designers, and product managers, the holistic understanding of the user needs becomes sharper, directly enhancing the UX.

MX as a bridge to comprehensive TX

Multiexperience acts as an important bridge between CX, EX, and UX, ensuring smooth interactions across all platforms. By investing in MX, businesses can create more connected and adaptive experiences that bring everything together.

Recent research predicts the Multi Experience Development Platforms market will grow by $4.67 billion by 2027, with a 21.9% CAGR.[8]

Effectively integrating Multiexperience sets the stage for a seamless and successful Total Experience strategy.

Critical reflections: Risks and barriers in Total Experience implementation

While Total Experience presents a promising approach to creating connected value across stakeholders, its implementation can be complex and context-dependent.

First, TX strategies are often presented in a positive light, may downplay real-world challenges. For instance, TX initiatives could introduce significant risks related to data governance, especially when integrating employee and

---

[7] *2017 State of Global Customer Service Report*, Microsoft, 2017. Based on interviews with 5,000 people from Brazil, Germany, Japan, the United Kingdom and the United States.

[8] *Global Multiexperience Development Platforms Market 2023-2027*, McKinsey & Well Company, 2023.

customer data streams. Ensuring ethical data usage, privacy compliance, and cybersecurity becomes essential.

Second, the idea that digital tools can seamlessly align internal and external experiences may underestimate organizational dynamics. Cultural misalignment, siloed departments, and resistance to change can all slow down progress. For organizations with lower digital maturity, the required infrastructure, such as AI platforms, Multiexperience interfaces, and integrated data environments, may be underdeveloped or financially out of reach, limiting broader adoption.

Finally, TX strategies can unintentionally increase the cognitive and operational load on employees. Automating workflows must be balanced with careful change management and employee empowerment to avoid burnout or disengagement.

Acknowledging these risks doesn't diminish the value of TX. Rather, it highlights the need for pragmatic planning, contextual awareness, and a phased, adaptive approach to implementation.

1.3. How to Implement a Total Experience Strategy

In an increasingly competitive market, delivering a smooth, interconnected experience across all touchpoints isn't just a nice-to-have; it's a necessity. But where do you start when building a Total Experience strategy that brings together Customer Experience, Employee Experience, User Experience, and Multiexperience?

Ask yourself:

- Are our customers' and employees' experiences truly aligned, or are we operating in silos?

- Do we have the right technology and data to deliver personalized, efficient interactions at every touchpoint?

- How can we adapt to ever-evolving needs, while remaining consistent across platforms?

These are just a few of the key questions to consider. To guide you through the process, let's look at a step-by-step framework for adopting a TX strategy.

Figure 1.2: A step-by-step guide to Total Experience strategy.

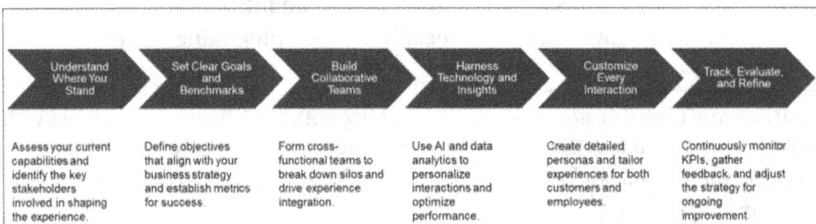

Understand Where You Stand	Set Clear Goals and Benchmarks	Build Collaborative Teams	Harness Technology and Insights	Customize Every Interaction	Track, Evaluate, and Refine
Assess your current capabilities and identify the key stakeholders involved in shaping the experience.	Define objectives that align with your business strategy and establish metrics for success.	Form cross-functional teams to break down silos and drive experience integration.	Use AI and data analytics to personalize interactions and optimize performance.	Create detailed personas and tailor experiences for both customers and employees.	Continuously monitor KPIs, gather feedback, and adjust the strategy for ongoing improvement.

Step 1: Assess the current state

Before committing to any major TX initiatives, it's important to know where you currently stand. This means taking a step back to understand how your organization manages CX, EX, UX, and MX.

- Map stakeholders: Identify everyone involved, from customers and employees to partners and users. Understanding your current experience will help you identify gaps and areas for improvement.

- Review processes: Look at how your teams currently handle customer support, employee engagement, and multi-platform experiences. This is a good time to collect any existing feedback or performance data.

- Audit your technology: Evaluate the current digital tools and platforms in use. Are they serving your needs, or are there areas where you could benefit from upgrades or better integration?

Step 2: Define clear objectives and success metrics

Once you have a clear picture of where you stand, it's time to set goals from where you want to go. What are the key outcomes you're hoping to achieve through TX?

- Align objectives with business goals: Make sure the TX objectives fit with your overall business strategies. For example, are you looking to increase customer engagement or boost employee engagement? Whatever your goals, they should support the larger organizational vision.

- Establish KPIs: Define specific, measurable KPIs across the CX, EX, UX, and MX dimensions to track your progress. For Customer Experience, consider metrics like customer satisfaction (CSAT), Net Promoter Score (NPS), churn rate or engagement indicators. For Employee Experience, look at employee engagement scores or retention rates. Usability metrics like click-through rates, task completion rates or time-on tasks could be considered for User Experience. Multiexperience might be measured by monitoring digital engagement metrics across devices and platforms. Regularly reviewing these KPIs will ensure your strategy stays aligned with both internal and external goals.

Step 3: Create cross-functional teams

A successful TX strategy doesn't work in silos. It requires collaboration across different departments.

- Build collaborative teams: Get representatives from marketing, sales, IT, HR, product development, customer support, and design together. Each time should work to achieve a common goal.

- Appoint an experience leader: If possible, assign a Chief Experience Officer (CXO) or someone else to lead the charge. This person will ensure that all initiatives stay consistent and aligned across different departments.

- Adopt agile processes: Use Agile methodologies to encourage rapid feedback and adaptation. The needs of both customers and employees change quickly, and agility will help you stay responsive.

Step 4: Leverage technology and data

The right technology can make or break your TX strategy. Data-driven insights will help you make smarter, faster decisions.

- Invest in integrated platforms: Implement AI-powered tools, CRM systems, Customer Data Platforms (CDP) and employee engagement platforms that pull data from multiple platforms into one place. This will allow you to see the big picture and deliver a more unified experience.

- Use Artificial Intelligence (AI) for personalization: AI can help tailor experiences for both customers and employees. By leveraging real-time insights, AI can provide personalized recommendations, streamline workflows, and improve overall engagement.

- Utilize data for continuous improvement: Data should drive your decisions. Analyze customer and employee behaviors to uncover patterns and areas for improvement. This will ensure you are evolving.

Step 5: Personalize the experience

Personalization is at the heart of Total Experience. It's what makes interactions feel relevant and meaningful.

- Develop detailed personas: Use the data you have gathered to create in-depth personas that reflect the needs, preferences, and challenges of both your customers and employees.

- Tailor the journey: Create personalized customer and employee journeys. This could mean offering more flexible work arrangements for employees or providing customized product recommendations for customers.

- Segment your audience: Group customers and employees into different segments to provide even more precise, targeted experiences. For instance, use customer data to send personalized product offers or employee data to recommend development programs.

Step 6: Continuously measure, analyze, and improve

Total Experience isn't a one-and-done initiative. It's a living, breathing strategy that evolves within your business and the needs of your stakeholders.

- Monitor your KPIs: Keep an eye on key performance indicators, like customer satisfaction and employee engagement. Regular tracking will ensure you are on the right path and can quickly adapt if necessary.

- Collect real-time feedback: Set up systems to gather feedback from customers and employees at critical touchpoints. Use surveys, focus groups, digital feedback forms, or sentiment analysis to continuously improve.

- Set up a governance model: Having the right governance in place is key. Make sure that data and feedback are shared not only with operational teams but also with key decision-makers. This ensures insights lead to action, rather than just becoming a theoretical exercise. Engaging leadership in this process helps drive accountability and alignment with organizational goals.

By following this framework and continuously evolving, your organization can create a truly interconnected Total Experience that benefits all the stakeholders involved.

From strategy to practice: framing the case studies

In the following sections, we present three case studies – Airbnb, Starbucks, and Tesla – that bring the Total Experience framework to life. These cases were selected to show how TX principles can be applied across different industries and organizational models. They are meant to be illustrative rather than exhaustive or statistically representative.

Each example offers valuable insights into how companies with different levels of digital maturity, operational complexity, and cultural readiness approach Total Experience. While they highlight successful practices, it's helpful to remember that what works in one context may not work in another. The goal is to offer inspiration and insight, rather than a fixed formula.

1.4. Airbnb's Smart Lock. A Case Study in Total Experience

Airbnb introduced smart lock integration in early 2023 as a pilot program, with a broader rollout planned from spring 2024.[9] This innovation was designed to streamline the check-in process for guests and simplify management for hosts, especially those with multiple listings or who do not live near their rental

---

[9] *Connect a smart lock to Airbnb for smoother check-ins.*, Airbnb, March 13, 2024. Available at: https://www.airbnb.com/resources/hosting-homes/a/connect-a-smart-lock-to-airbnb-for-smoother-check-ins-667?_set_bev_on_new_domain=1714574330_Z jA0NmE4OWJhMWI4&locale=en

properties. The service is available in the US and Canada, with plans to expand to other countries and include more smart locks in the future.

Airbnb's smart locks allow hosts to connect compatible electronic locks to their Airbnb accounts. This system automatically generates and shares unique access codes with guests for each new booking. It enhances security by ensuring that codes are only active during the booked stay, and it provides a seamless check-in experience without the need for physical keys.

Airbnb's adoption of smart locks is an example of a Total Experience strategy that effectively enhances Customer Experience, Employee Experience, User Experience, and Multiexperience.

Impact on Customer Experience

- The introduction of smarts locks significantly enhances guest convenience by allowing self-service check-in and check-out. This eliminates the need for coordinating schedules with hosts for key exchanges, thereby reducing wait times and potential stress, leading to higher guest satisfaction. Guests feel more in control of their stay, as they are able to access the property independently, which is particularly beneficial for late arrivals or when social distancing is necessary.

- Hosts can manage property access remotely, reducing the need for physical presence for key exchanges. This is especially useful for hosts managing multiple properties or those who live far from their rental units. Hosts benefit from increased flexibility and from reduced direct interaction, saving time and minimizing scheduling conflicts.

The system also offers hosts peace of mind regarding key security, as it eliminates the risk associated with lost keys or unauthorized copies or access. According to Airbnb, "Hosts in North America who added smart lock integration in early testing have an average check-in rating of 4.95."[10]

Impact on Employee Experience

- Customer service and operations: For Airbnb employees, particularly those in customer service and operations, smart lockers streamline the support process. With fewer incidents of guests unable to access accommodations due to missing or unavailable hosts, there is a reduction in emergency support calls and complaints. This alleviates pressure on customer service teams, allowing them to focus on more complex queries, thus improving overall job satisfaction.

---

[10] Ibid. Based on listings with a smart lock connected to Airbnb between January 1 and June 30, 2024.

- Back office and operational activities: The automation of key exchanges simplifies many operational processes. For example, logistics related to key handovers are minimized, which reduces the workload on employees managing property listings and host accounts. The data collected from these interactions can also provide valuable insights for operational improvements and strategic planning.

Influence on User Experience

- Seamless integration: The smart lock system is integrated within the Airbnb app, where guests can receive and access their entry codes. This solution keeps all necessary information in one place, reducing confusion and the potential for errors.

- Reliability: The UX is designed to ensure that even if there are connectivity issues with the lock, guests can use backup codes or alternative methods of entry, which are also managed through the app.

Changes in Multiexperience

- Consistency across channels: Smart locks integrate into Airbnb's broader MX strategy by providing a consistent and unified User Experience across various digital and physical touchpoints. Whether accessing instructions via the app, website, or receiving notifications, the experience remains seamless across all platforms.

- Support from chatbot assistance: Chatbots enhance the MX by offering consistent, helpful support across multiple digital channels. They assist guests with smart lock access and troubleshoot issues, which reduces the need for live agent intervention and streamlines the service experience. This integration ensures that, regardless of the touch point, guests receive timely and effective support, maintaining a high level of service quality across all interactions.

- Integration with other services: Smart lock integration works seamlessly with other Airbnb services, like automated check-in instructions and customer support chatbots, providing a holistic service experience.

The implementation of smart locks by Airbnb is a strategic enhancement that positively affects all aspects of the Total Experience. It simplifies and secures the check-in process, reduces operational burdens, and integrates digital advancements to improve both Customer and Employee Experiences. This innovation not only boosts CX by facilitating smoother guest and host interactions but also enriches EX by optimizing workflows and reducing stress on customer service teams. In UX and MX, it ensures a seamless, cohesive journey across all touchpoints, reinforcing Airbnb's commitment to a holistic and satisfying User Experience.

1.5. Starbucks and the Clover Vertica. Brewing Innovation for Total Experience

Starbucks introduced the Clover Vertica brewing machine in 2022 as part of its ongoing commitment to elevate coffee craft and drive innovation. The machine utilizes proprietary technology to brew freshly ground coffee in just 30 seconds, making it the fastest bean-to-cup experience in the industry. By eliminating paper filters and using precise brewing techniques, Clover Vertica contributes to Starbucks' goals of reducing waste and cutting water and carbon usage by 50% by 2030.[11] The machine will be fully deployed across all US stores by 2025 as part of Starbucks' broader strategy to enhance operational efficiency and customer satisfaction.[12]

This innovation showcases how Starbucks integrates cutting-edge solutions to transform the Total Experience, impacting in distinct and valuable ways:

Customer Experience

- Freshness and quality: The machine uses proprietary technology to brew coffee one cup at a time, using freshly ground beans. This method ensures that every cup is made to order and offers peak freshness, a key factor in flavor and quality that coffee enthusiasts highly value.

- Speed and efficiency: It brews a cup of coffee in just 30 seconds, dramatically reducing wait times compared to traditional brewing methods. This efficiency is particularly beneficial during peak hours, improving service speed and reducing lines, and therefore lifting overall satisfaction.

- Customization: Clover Vertica allows for a high degree of customization. Customers can choose from a variety of beans, and the machine's precise control over brewing parameters (like water temperature and brew time) means that each cup can be tailored to individual preferences. This capability aligns well with the growing consumer demand for personalized experiences.

- Customer engagement: The use of such advanced technology in stores can also provide an educational component for customers who are interested in the specifics of coffee brewing. Baristas can share

---

[11] *Day 6: Innovating for the Future,* Starbucks Stories and News, September 29, 2023. Available at: Day 6: Innovating for the Future - Starbucks Stories.

[12] *Starbucks Showcases Innovation for Growth and a More Connected and Sustainable Future at 2022 Meeting Stakeholders,* Starbucks Stories and News, March 16, 2022. Available at: Starbucks Showcases Innovation for Growth and a More Connected and Sustainable Future at 2022 Annual Meeting.

insights about the different beans available and how variations in the brewing process affect taste, creating a more engaging and informative experience.

- Consistency: With automated technology, Clover Vertica ensures that each cup of coffee is consistent in quality and taste. This reliability can enhance customer trust and satisfaction, as fans can expect the same high-quality brew with every visit.

- Environmental impact: The machine's efficiency not only applies to time but also to the optimization of resources, such as coffee beans and water, reducing waste. This aspect appeals to environmentally conscious consumers who prioritize sustainability in their purchasing decisions.

Employee Experience

- Reduced physical strain: Traditional coffee brewing can be labor-intensive, especially during peak hours. The Clover Vertica automates the brewing process, reducing the physical effort required from baristas. This can help minimize fatigue and physical strain, leading to a more comfortable work environment.

- Efficiency and workflow: By speeding up the coffee brewing process, Clover Vertica allows baristas to manage their time and tasks more efficiently. This efficiency can lead to a smoother workflow and less stress, as employees can handle high volumes of orders more effectively without sacrificing quality.

- Skill development: While the machine automates much of the brewing process, it also offers opportunities for baristas to learn about advanced coffee technology and brewing techniques. This can enhance their skills and knowledge, making their job more engaging and potentially opening further career opportunities within the coffee industry.

- Customer interaction: With less time needed for coffee preparation, baristas can spend more time interacting with customers, enhancing service quality and personal connection. This not only improves the Customer Experience but can also make the job more fulfilling for employees, as they have more opportunities to engage positively with patrons.

- Consistency and pride in product: The Clover Vertica ensures a consistent, high-quality product with every brew, which helps baristas feel confident in the coffee they serve, enhancing job satisfaction, and allows them to take pride in the reliability and quality of the product they offer.

User Experience

- Digital interface: Clover Vertica machines typically feature sophisticated digital interfaces that allow baristas to interact with the machine in a more intuitive and engaging way. For customers, the ability to see the options available, such as coffee type, grind settings, and brewing times, can demystify the brewing process and enhance the overall experience through transparency.

- Enhanced interaction: The experience of watching their coffee brewed on demand through systems like Clover Vertica adds an element of theater to the coffee shop visit. The fast production of coffee ensures that customers spend less time waiting, enhancing their overall in-store experience.

- Customization at the touch of a button: The digital interface of the Clover Vertica enables easy customization of coffee orders. Users can adjust settings like brewing strength and temperature to suit their personal taste preferences, directly through touchscreen panels or indirectly through barista input. This level of control makes the coffee experience highly personalized and user-centered.

Multiexperience

- Digital integration: These technologies are likely integrated with Starbucks' digital systems, allowing for smoother operation and better inventory management. For instance, knowing the exact amount of coffee used can help with stock predictions and management, which feeds back into the mobile app for better customer updates on product availability.

- Consistent quality across touchpoints: Whether ordering via the app, at a drive-thru, or in-store, these technologies ensure that the quality of the beverage is consistent, no matter how the customer chooses to interact with Starbucks. This consistency is crucial for maintaining trust and satisfaction across various service platforms.

These innovations show Starbucks' commitment to improving every facet of the interaction chain, from brewing to final delivery, enhancing the experience for all users involved, directly and indirectly.

1.6. Tesla's Holistic Approach to Total Experience

Tesla is often hailed as one of the world's most innovative companies, not just for its electric vehicles but for the comprehensive, experience-driven ecosystem it has built for customers, employees, and users. The company's strategy goes beyond delivering cutting-edge products; it focuses on creating an integrated experience that seamlessly connects all touchpoints — from the moment a potential customer first engages with the brand to long-term ownership and service interactions. This approach reflects Tesla's commitment to delivering consistent, customer-centric value, aligning every aspect of the journey with its broader mission of innovation and sustainability.

Tesla's direct-to-consumer model, use of digital tools, and advanced technology solutions allow the company to create a cohesive experience that transforms how people interact with their vehicles and the brand itself. From simplifying the car-buying process to ensuring continuous software upgrades, Tesla demonstrates a deep understanding of the evolving needs of both customers and employees, making it a leader in Total Experience strategy. By controlling every stage of the customer journey and empowering its workforce with the latest tools and training, Tesla has not only redefined the auto industry but also set a new standard for how businesses can align customer and employee experiences to drive loyalty and long-term success.

Customer Experience

The company has revolutionized the car-buying process by eliminating traditional dealerships. Customers can order vehicles entirely online, making the buying process transparent, streamlined, and free from the pressure of sales tactics. Tesla's commitment to customer satisfaction is evident in its Supercharger network, which achieved an impressive 99.97% uptime in 2023, ensuring that customers always have reliable access to charging stations.[13]

In showrooms, the emphasis is not on hard selling but on educating and immersing customers in the brand's technology and innovation. Visitors are encouraged to interact with the vehicles and configure their choices in real-time, creating a hands-on, immersive buying experience.

Employee Experience

This innovative brand recognizes that engaged and empowered employees are key to delivering superior customer service. Staff members are equipped with advanced digital tools like tablets that provide real-time access to inventory, vehicle configurations, and financing options, enabling them to offer faster and more accurate assistance to customers.

This investment in digital tools and continuous employee training ensures that the workforce is aligned with Tesla's broader mission of sustainability and innovation, fostering a strong sense of engagement and purpose.

---

[13] *Impact Report*, Tesla, 2023.

User Experience

Tesla has made vehicle ownership incredibly user-friendly, thanks largely to the app, which allows users to monitor charging status, unlock the car remotely, and control various functions, always adding a layer of convenience.

A key feature of the user experience is the large central touchscreen, which consolidates controls for everything, from navigation to entertainment, simplifying vehicle management. Over-the-air software updates continuously improve the vehicle's performance and add new features, ensuring the experience evolves without requiring service visits.

Multiexperience

Tesla combines the physical and digital aspects of its business in a way that creates a unified experience. Whether customers are purchasing a vehicle, scheduling a service, or charging their car during a road trip, the company ensures consistency across all touchpoints.

The mobile app bridges the gap between the physical product (the car) and the digital ecosystem, allowing customers to design and purchase their vehicle online with real-time updates. Mobile service units and an extensive charging network further enhance the MX, providing a seamless, frictionless ownership experience. Real-time charging availability and route planning are integrated into the car's navigation system, offering a smooth and connected driving experience.

Key takeaways from Tesla's TX Strategy

- Holistic customer journey: The company unifies digital tools, physical products, and service touchpoints, ensuring a consistent and integrated customer journey that eliminates frictions and strengthens engagement and loyalty.

- Adaptive product lifecycle: Over-the-air updates continuously improve vehicles, allowing them to evolve over time. This innovative approach extends product longevity and enhances ownership satisfaction.

- Direct-to-consumer approach: Owning every stage of the customer journey provides a personalized, transparent experience, unmatched by traditional dealerships, resulting in faster decision-making and increased customer trust.

- Empowered workforce for superior service: The company's investment in employee empowerment and development not only drives internal efficiency but also enhances the Customer Experience. By equipping staff with the right tools and knowledge, the company ensures that every customer interaction reflects its values of innovation, sustainability, and service excellence.

- Sustainability as a core experience: Tesla's ability to avoid 20 million metric tons of CO_2 emissions in 2023 highlights the company's alignment between sustainability and Customer Experience, making ownership a more environmentally conscious choice for customers.[14]

1.7. Conclusion. The Strategic Impact of Total Experience

Incorporating a Total Experience strategy not only unifies Customer, Employee, User, and Multiexperience domains but also drives substantial value across all aspects of business operations. In more detail, TX leads to:

Enhanced brand consistency: A TX strategy ensures that every interaction with the brand, whether internal or external, online or offline, delivers a consistent message and quality. This consistency solidifies the brand's identity and reputation, fostering trust among all stakeholders.

Operational efficiency: TX breaks down the silos between different departments, leading to more streamlined operations. This integration increases efficiency, reduces costs, and improves service delivery, all of which contribute to a more agile business.

Increased innovation: By facilitating better communication and collaboration across various teams, a TX approach encourages innovation that can significantly enhance product and service offerings, directly influencing competitive advantage.

Greater stakeholder satisfaction: Focusing holistically on the experiences of employees, customers, and users leads to increased satisfaction levels across the board. Satisfied employees are more engaged and productive, which enhances the quality of customer interactions, leading to higher customer loyalty.

Agility and responsiveness: Companies with a robust Total Experience framework can adapt more swiftly to market changes and customer needs, ensuring they remain relevant and competitive in a fast-paced market.

Sustainability: Implementing TX strategies often leads to more sustainable business practices. For example, streamlined operations can reduce waste and resource use, while sustainable innovations in product and service development can attract eco-conscious consumers.

1.8 Limitations and Scope of Application

While the Total Experience framework holds strong strategic potential, it doesn't work the same for every organization. TX strategies are most effective in organizations that:

---

[14] Ibid.

- Have a mature digital infrastructure and strong data analytics capabilities.

- Operate across multiple customer and employee interaction channels.

- Embrace cross-functional collaboration and agile governance models.

On the other hand, companies with limited tech integrations, poor collaboration or strict hierarchies may struggle to apply TX smoothly. Also, TX works best when people, both inside and outside the company, are open to working together and trying out new ideas.

This book doesn't offer a one-size-fits-all solution; it provides a way of thinking and seeing experience as something connected, dynamic, and worth shaping.

Leaders should take a close look at their own organization's readiness, tech capabilities, and company culture before rolling out TX strategies on a large scale.

Bibliography

2017 State of Global Customer Service Report, Microsoft, 2017

Burke, Brian. *Top Strategic Technology Trends for 2021*, Gartner, 2020. Gartner is a trademark of Gartner, Inc. and/or its affiliates. This Gartner report is archived and is included for historical context only.

Chandra, Das Avinash, Greg Phalin, Ishwar Lal Patidar, Malcolm Gomes, Rakshit Sawhney, and Renny Thomas. *The next frontier of customer engagement: AI-enabled customer service*, McKinsey 2023.

Connect a smart lock to Airbnb for smoother check-ins., Airbnb, March 13, 2024. Available at: https://www.airbnb.com/resources/hosting-homes/a/connect-a-smart-lock-to-airbnb-for-smoother-check-ins-667?_set_bev_on_new_domain=1714574330_ZjA0NmE4OWJhMWI4&locale=en

Day 6: Innovating for the Future, Starbucks Stories and News, September 29, 2023. Available at: Day 6: Innovating for the Future - Starbucks Stories.

Global Multi-experience Development Platforms Market 2023-2027, McKinsey & Well Company, 2023.

Impact Report, Tesla, 2023.

State of the American Workplace, Gallup, 2017.

Starbucks Showcases Innovation for Growth and a More Connected and Sustainable Future at 2022 Meeting Stakeholders, Starbucks Stories and News, March 16, 2022. Available at: Starbucks Showcases Innovation for Growth and a More Connected and Sustainable Future at 2022 Annual Meeting.

Top Strategic Technology Trends for 2022. 12 Trends Shaping the Future of Digital Business, Gartner, 2021. This Gartner report is archived and is included for historical context only.

Chapter Two
From Total Experience to Total Marketing

Frank Pagano

I know this may sound self-centered, especially from the voice of someone who sells technology, but the more meetings and projects I go through, the more I see that, once we have figured out what the business goals are for the year – say, together with Client A, or for the short and long term, then it all starts with technology. And that means going digital and fully embracing exponential technologies, like blockchain and artificial intelligence. Digital transformation initiatives are, indeed, the foundation of Total Marketing. Tech kicks in exactly when the C-room starts asking: 'All clear, but how do we do that, profitably and pragmatically?'.

What is the relevance of technology, anyway? Or, verbalized in a simpler way, why do we bother with it? The main purpose of tech is to enable a more connected, efficient, and responsive experience for all stakeholders, be them external or internal to a firm.

The list of all digital properties, social media accounts, platforms to interact with fans, suppliers and employees, plus the various databases where we store data: all of it should be visible to management, intentional in its role and fully utilized. In the end, the hardware & software tools of a company, called its tech stack, are the first step of any conversation regarding the execution of the company's plans. This doesn't mean that technology is more important than strategy or people, be they consumers, partners, or own team members. And it's more than just a discussion about tools. The function of tech, to say it in a different way, is to get continuous, accurate and swift feedback from physical and digital touchpoints, and to respond to any stakeholder as fast as possible, empowering anyone with what they need and with the maximum personalization possible.

In this chapter, we will look at some successful total experiences (or, as close as possible to Gartner's Total Experience framework) based on conscious decisions and perfect management of exponential technologies. The question is: what does marketing look like, considering the multiple experiences unveiled by "the Gartner model." If Total Marketing exists, what are the new 4 Ps[1]? It's usually a slow build to get to the destination of a full digital transformation, and it requires continuous improvement and progressively perfected execution. We will see that exponential technologies have the intrinsic ability to radically transform the basics, namely the marketing mix.

So, here is a bit of theory, before diving into real-life cases. And, even before that, a small note on blockchain may be appropriate.

2.1. Are We Still Talking About Blockchain?

Artificial intelligence (AI) has become everyone's hero. There is no public debate, meeting, or quarterly results call from listed companies without frequent mentions of some AI strategies, which will revolutionize our world. So, why is blockchain mentioned among the items to be kept on our radar?

We could not write about blockchain, and the more general Web3 topic, without acknowledging that the media bubble around the metaverse, cryptocurrencies and NFTs (Non-Fungible Tokens) has burst violently. However, looking at the yearly 'State of Crypto' reports[2] from a16z, an investment fund[3], nothing has changed for developers and industry veterans of distributed ledgers (another name for blockchains), especially from an enterprise or B2B perspective.

The army of speculators and day-traders, that's for sure, has abandoned the ship. Fortunately, one might say. But, if we observe the underlying growth signals, such as the number of blockchain projects or active wallets, or other Web3 adoption metrics, real-life use cases continue to grow (we are still talking about niche penetration, to be fully transparent – no pun intended with blockchain's transparency feature). Less media and speculative pressures allow companies to focus on what this technology does best: creating efficiencies and increasing people's engagement.

---

[1] The famous 4 P-s of marketing, also known as marketing mix, are product, price, placement and promotion. The model dates to the 1950s and was popularized by the 'Godfather' of modern marketing, Professor Philip Kotler.

[2] The State of Crypto Index, from a16z, is an invaluable resource to monitor the development of the crypto space and the adoption of blockchains globally. The Index is based on multiple variables, whole sources are verified, and it is continuously updated. Please, refer to https://a16zcrypto.com/stateofcrypto/.

[3] The fund belongs to Andreessen and Horowitz, whose two founders are among the most respected figures in Silicon Valley. The broader fund manages approximately $34 Bill in assets, and it invests in various fields across tech, gaming, AI, health, fin-tech, and many more. It's not among the largest funds in the world, but it produces best-in-class research and reports.

To clear the field from misunderstandings, by Web3, we mean an evolution of the Internet into a new era, where two things will happen:

1. The physical and the digital worlds will merge, thanks to the new frontiers of software and hardware (see the case of smart goggles by Apple or Meta, and their augmented reality features). This will make any experience, including the daily dialogue with a brand, whether you are a supplier or a fan, increasingly immersive.

2. The ownership of someone's digital agency is returned to the individuals, while the rewards are fairly distributed among companies, intermediaries, and consumers, as they are now tracked and acted against in a programmable way, which is linked to blockchain's native payment rails.[4]

To put it more bluntly, a physical store and the e-commerce of the same company are usually two silos, with very few communication bridges; and e-commerce is always presented to fans in a two-dimensional way. Moreover, data and rewards for interactions on Facebook, Instagram or Amazon, for example, are captured by the platform owners, without exception. The average fee extracted on investments made on creators' content (say, a branded advertising message or a pre-roll) goes from 45% at YouTube (belonging to Alphabet) up to 100% for the Meta-owned apps.[5]

The evolution of digital infrastructure, from Web3 to metaverses, all based on blockchain, will take by storm the way any brand and company converses with people and their network. What's new in the consumer, employee and supplier journey? What's different in the sales ritual and the dialogue between the brand and its users?

Blockchain will become mainstream by 2030, at least according to consulting firms and experts monitoring its penetration curves around the world.[6] Indeed, giants such as LVMH, Starbucks, Visa, or Siemens are integrating blockchain

---

[4] The benchmark guide about Web3 is Matthew Ball, *The Metaverse: Fully Revised and Updated Edition: Building the Spatial Internet*, Liveright, 2024.

[5] A great source of information on the topic of digital agency and fair compensation is Animoca Brands' website, www.animocabrands.com, which is a fund and a platform, whose vision is to "to deliver digital property rights to consumers around the world to help to establish the open metaverse." Animoca is the driving force behind unicorn metaverses like The Sandbox.

[6] Reading articles and reports from the likes of McKinsey or The Economist will show a convergence towards 2030 as a turning point for the adoption of exponential technologies like blockchain. The date is believed to be the beginning of the decline of the purchasing power of Boomers and Gen X-ers, with the vast majority of purchasing power controlled by new generations (Z and Alpha).

into their processes and reinventing the relationships with fans. The efficiency, tracking, and reconciliation properties of blockchain will help to disrupt the 4 Ps model. Business will not be the same if we have an infrastructure that tracks and acts against digital agency, with programmable compensation for engagement. Therefore, blockchain is an essential piece of this puzzle.

Now, what will marketing look like in five years, thanks to exponential technologies like AI and blockchain? Here's the answer, in a nutshell.

It will move from pure product to meta-product; from standardized pricing to customized and dynamic rates; from exchange of ownership to renting, and fluid trading brand-to-fan and fan-to-fan; and from storytelling to co-creation of social capital, within a narrative that nurtures the mutual interest between user and brand. The marketing mix will never be the same.

Who is the biggest loser? The great hero of the last seventy years, namely the 'Mad Man,' from the famous Netflix series, or the omnipotent company leader and manager. The human CEO is dead, so to speak. Long live a new CEO, whose powers are augmented by machines. A few examples in the second half of this chapter will help.

2.2. Nothing Personal?

No hard feelings. We should leave emotions at the door, as we kiss goodbye to traditional marketing. Blockchain and AI will allow us to finally realize what marketing always wanted to do: efficiently give people what they want, as if the brand proposition were made just for them, one by one, and at that very moment. It is the dream of absolute personalization. Tech will make it possible, finally.

Individualization of marketing will become the dominant business model. All we need to do is to reverse the traditional journey (the so-called consumer funnel), which was designed as an epic, linear ride from awareness to consideration, to purchase, as if fans were drowning into a vicious spiral, firmly controlled by the distribution and communication oligopoly, ruled by TV, large chains and digital platforms. The 'Mad Men' made us listen to their message and buy their products, sharing their profits mainly with distribution, thanks to a commercial mark-up ranging from 30 to 50 percent of the retail price, depending on the industry. This illusion of freedom of choice was also called "love" for the brand or *Lovemark*, to quote Kevin Roberts' ultra-famous book[7]. It wasn't. It was, in fact, the outcome of a dictatorship. In this equation, the product was always the weak link: created in a linear fashion (produce, sell,

---

[7] The book by Roberts is a true marketing bible. Here it is: Kevin Roberts, *Lovemarks*, powerHouse Books, 2005. It educated a whole generation of marketing professionals and top executives, until the mid 2010s.

trash), and with all externalities pushed out to governments and future generations. Employees, partners, and suppliers never really had a place in this framework. What about the broader world? Is what's going on behind the scenes relevant to fans?

The new funnel of the brand-consumer dialogue redistributes the resources of the profit and loss accounts first to the fans, to the 'we,' the people, and reverses the linear model, producing physical products only when and where they are needed, and with an exponential and finally positive impact on the environment. Moreover, the purchase of a physical product will not be at the end of a straight line. Sometimes, the purchase will not even happen[8]. Archrival, a research institution and agency focused on new generations, states in their latest report of Gen Z and their relationship with brands: "in the old world, brands were at the center of the consumer journey — today, people are (and, you could argue, always should have been)."[9]

Welcome to a new world, with four completely new Ps. Employees, suppliers, and fans will share feedback and other relevant information at each touchpoint, keeping their privacy intact, to continuously give input and receive output, using only the needed resources for that inflow and outflow of contributions. Without data pooling, data governance, data crunching, and informed action against it, it would be too labor- and energy-intensive to give birth to efficiency and impact in any value-added proposition for all individuals. Think about it: billions of transactions per day, going through the refinery of AI, which finds meaning in a chaos of zeros and ones. It was inconceivable until this very day. The table below can help summarize what will change.

Technology is very much like a modern Peter Pan, stealing from concentrated 'old money,' to give power back to the network. We are not making a value or moral judgment here. The purpose of the table is to describe a likely shift, which is enabled by new tech capabilities and driven by the imperative of the best use of available resources. The truth is that we need everyone, their data, and their actions, physically and digitally, to thrive as brands and local and global communities. Adding employees and suppliers to the equation multiplies value, or the pie that we all eat. The modern Peter Pan doesn't play a zero-sum game. There is a new market in town: making sense of the data around us.

---

[8] A very compelling read on this topic is: *Gen Z Broke the Marketing Funnel*, Vogue Business, Archrival, 2024. For more information, see: www.genzbrokethefunnel.com. Archrival calls itself a "Youth Culture Agency," as you can see here: www.archrival.com.

[9] *Gen Z Broke the Marketing Funnel*, Vogue Business, Archrival, 2024.

Table 2.1: Total Marketing, with its new 4 Ps.

The 4 P's	Average % of Gross Sales	What will change in the future, thanks to technology?
Product	20-30	Speed up and streamline operations: optimize input from & towards employees and suppliers; eliminate black and counterfeit markets; certify the narrative of a sustainable and transparent supply chain; create a digital-first supply chain; everything has a digital twin. Sell it: digitally, and then in the physical world, ideally on demand; what sticks becomes the new core; progressive transition from standardized products to unique ones, made to order and on an individual basis, especially for novelties. Entertaining wins over producing: Win the minds and the hearts of fans; experiences, digital and immersive, to accompany any physical product proposition.
Price & Distribution	35	Eliminate standardized discounts and aggressive *'urbi et orbi'* trade marketing tactics, making the company's profit and loss accounts efficient through on-demand and *ad personam* individual and private benefit sharing, managed by AI and smart contracts. Disburse dynamic and customized value propositions, based on someone's history and social capital: for fans, and for employees and suppliers, when they deliver service excellence. Rebalance rent vs. ownership: everything is resalable at a certified residual value, tracked on public blockchains, with no information asymmetry.
Promotion	10-15	Transform the dialogue with fans & the broader network of suppliers & agencies into a one-to-one interaction, managed by data, analytics and AI, and executed on public blockchains, for transparency of process and content. Dissolve omnichannel into a blockchain, AI and digitally powered spatial reality - or a digitally immersive context; it is a convergence of technologies and hybrid realities. Democratize brands, making equity liquid, almost like a currency, in the hands of people, from fans to employees, from agencies to the long list of suppliers: everyone is a partner; boost collaboration between the brand and its full network of stakeholders, to increase mutual social capital: storytelling ceases to be one-sided.

Here is a small note for the fans of the 4 Ps model: We are not questioning a model that seemed and still seems to work, as it informs so many enterprise discussions about what they do every day. Our point is to add depth and width to the traditional 4 Ps, thanks to data and the technology that allows us to make sense of it and to create suggestions for management on how to better engage with consumers, while building a strong network of employees, suppliers and stakeholders. It's 4 Ps on steroids, to make it a bit more colorful. We are not after Professor Kotler's baby. We are after larger profit pools for all.

2.3. Product and Its Alter Ego

Any innovation is a risky bet. Heavy market research protocols are needed to design product and service proposals that can attract a defined, and more importantly, numerous, target audience. The process helps to sweeten decisions on the CapEx necessary to bring the innovation to life. These are usually multimillion-dollar checks to create factories or additional supply chain sourcing streams. So far, so good. The only problem is that, over the past two decades, big corporate innovation centers have failed miserably relative to their promises, as reported, for example, by the well-known consulting firm Capgemini.[10]

The reality is complex, and generational changes are occurring in parallel with telluric transformations in media and commerce. The only solution to hedge against the uncertainty that has become so common, after a couple of roller-coaster years of COVID-19, is to produce everything digitally and distribute innovation via digital twins, directly into the wallets (or pockets) of present and future fans. Advances in 3D design and the opportunity to use the virtues of blockchain are the drivers of the exponentially cheaper, one-to-one dialogue with every fan. Here is the potential turnkey. Product innovation must begin as a 'digital twin' or 'digital passport,' containing all the specifics of a brand's proposition, plus the benefits and rights of ultra-personalization, with blockchain as the infrastructure of choice to build trust, track engagement between brand and fan, and manage payments. The physical product will always follow the meta-product, that is, its digital version, which carries rights and benefits in its belly, and which brand and fans will share at the beginning of their journey.

---

[10] We are referring here to a report issued by Capgemini's Digital Transformation Institute in December of 2017, titled *The discipline of innovation: making sure your innovation center actually makes your organization more innovative*. The document highlights how corporations invest in large innovation centers and yet struggle to become more innovative. There are plenty of reports that stress similar limitations of the traditional, global corporate innovation centers.

Let's make an example. The luxury watch brand Audemars Piguet[11] could start considering how many new Royal Oaks, their flagship silhouette, to produce in an upgraded version. Since nobody can predict the success of a new model, the brand could decide to disseminate digital twins of a new watch, on a marketplace or via email to their database of collectors first, and read the demand digitally, based on how many digital watches were placed and paid for. Fans would get a preview of the new model and interact, with the use of an AI bot, to tweak and customize their watches, potentially with different prices, just as only an old-world *bottega* would do. For example, how many of these watches can sport a $1 million diamond on the dial? We wouldn't know until we asked the potential buyer or buyers. Finally, the brand would ship the product to the door, individually, against payments made long before, zeroing any risk of bad inventory and forecast misalignment. If a specific model is not only liked but consistently asked for digitally, then it will enter the brand's permanent assortment, always accompanied by its digital twin, which is registered on the chain. In addition, digital twins will contain the history of the entire supply chain, from start to finish, by law, to give transparency about what the brand does, and how it treats suppliers, employees and networks. This feat would fully meet the requirements of the digital passport regulation, which was approved in the EU in 2024.[12] This new way of innovating will make the luxury world sustainable, and drastically reduce counterfeiting and the black market, which is estimated to be as large as the official one. The deterministic nature of blockchain and a dialogue brand – fan powered by AI will make our production and suppliers' management more efficient, as smart contracts can zero all human errors; and AI makes sure fans get the level of personalization that is both feasible and that they deserve. This is the beauty of automation.

An important *caveat* is due here. This example does not mean that we should flip all supply chains. Toilet paper, for example, will continue to be produced

---

[11] This is a hypothetical example, to use a known luxury brand for accessories. The use case is compelling, because we are focusing on a brand that leverages scarcity and has a well curated database of high-net-worth individuals at a global level.

[12] We are referring here to what is known as *Eco-design for Sustainable Products Regulation*, or Regulation (EU) 2024/1781 of the European Parliament and of the EU Council, of June 13th, 2024, establishing a framework for the setting of eco-design requirements for sustainable products, which would entail the presence of a digital passport for every product being sold in Europe. It is expected to become national law across Europe by early 2027. In more detail, the "digital product passport," or DPP, will store relevant product information, including raw materials and their origin, recycling capabilities and lifecycle environmental impact, to substantiate products' sustainability claims, promote their circularity and strengthen legal compliance. For more information, see: https://ceoworld.biz/2025/05/21/who-made-my-stuff-just-ask-its-digital-product-passport-dpp/.

en masse. The point is that we can inject technology into complex supply chains, creating digital twins of entire value chains, with their vast network of suppliers and pricey raw materials (COGS,) and optimize the backend, while surprising and delighting users. This will boost efficiency and sales. Fans will want to know that a watch is original, and that its supply is certified, with world-class standards, and have that data right in their digital twins. Fans have the incentive to track product usage, which makes the residual value of the watch certain, and which represents pure gold for the manufacturer and its suppliers. If we were Audemars Piguet, we would want to know if a watch spring has a manufacturing defect, as my reputation is built on excellence and perfection. This is where tech can help. Question: How much should fans pay for all this customization, compared to a product that is usually standardized? The answer is: it depends.

2.4. The Price Is Right?

It depends, as mentioned. A super-fan, who helps their favorite brand innovate, should get financial perks and incentives, which can be used, for example, for personalized discounts or access to unique experiences. Blockchains represent the public registry of the activities of a network of brand ambassadors, who get rewarded through the same tangible resources, which would traditionally go into discounts and commercial mark-ups for large distribution chains. The dissemination of incentives could extend to employees and suppliers, rewarding virtuous behaviors and excellent service levels.

Product innovation, as a first step, should flow first to super-fans, who do not have to wait in line to get their goodies. If I am an Apple fanatic, who has stayed with the brand since the 1980s, why should I be given the same statistical probability to receive my new iPhone as a one-timer or a newbie, for example, by queuing for hours on 5th Avenue in New York or trying my luck online, when the brand starts taking orders? Why should I be on a distribution list with hundreds of thousands of people, who may not have the same loyalty record and are simply divided into clusters or tiers decided by the headquarters? I would like to be treated differently, as my history is unique. The problem is that, until now, this would be too labor-intensive, without exponential tech.

The community of true *aficionados* will help the brand to spread the word about innovation and should be rewarded for it. Digital twins will contain concrete benefits, proportionally calculated by AI, and linked to the engagement history of each fan, which is finally transparent and accurate. You can almost bid farewell to the standardized pricing system: pricing will become fluid, as if every product or service were a financial product. We have the right technology for this. The fan is at the center of it all and will no longer need to wait for the brand to give them hard discounts during the next Black Friday craze. Fans will exchange and share perks and points earned, in complete security and privacy. Blockchains and AI will finally tie prices to the objective value of various brand offerings in the eyes of one specific consumer, given their history and the value for money that they are looking for. The most creative and exciting products will be able to see their price explode, with brands continually reaping the benefits of an endless vortex of brand-fan-fan exchange. The number one commercial goal throughout the year will not be to sell more boxes before Christmas than the year before, or not just that. Top-line growth will be the natural result of another growing imperative, which is the creation of shared value for the community, in its broadest sense. Top-line growth will finally be detached from COGS, material costs, and production, making ours a more sustainable world. Most sales will remain digital, as they are designed exclusively for a digital world, where our avatars or agents can enjoy 3D shoes, services, or virtual events.

Just to be clear, we are not talking about a roll-out of dynamic pricing, which will remain a feature within selected industries, or the death of standardized pricing. We don't advocate for the removal, for example, of the European Fair Competition law, giving permission to manufacturers to do whatever they please with pricing. [13] Airlines and holiday packages are usually sold via dynamic pricing (prices on a Tuesday may differ from those on Wednesday, for a million reasons, like occupancy rates, popularity of the journey and destination, and number of days to departure; all managed via simple algorithms,) as we know, and this will not change, as it is a part of their DNA as businesses. Events, like concerts, have a tiered approach to seats and a solid secondary market, which may or may not be disciplined by the organizers. Grocery stores have loyalty programs, where members enjoy everyday favorable rates. Luxury retailers, especially for accessories, pass VIP discounts to their best collectors at their discretion (it's a world-known secret.) Cash-back is the usual formula for most credit card operators. All fashion e-commerce outlets offer first-time visitors a welcome discount in exchange for their email and permission to send a newsletter. All these examples don't require exponential technologies and are mechanical enablers of higher sales and engagement. What's different in the case of exponential technologies is the ability to track someone's loyalty on chain and to act against it at a global level, to sell digitally first, via digital twins, with payments, perks and commitments managed via smart contracts, and to inject AI into mix, so that a chat-bot or an avatar could discuss directly and on a one-to-one basis with each customer,

---

[13] For the EU fair competition legislation, including price fixing, see: www.european-union.europa.eu.

landing on a price that is customized, in line with local rules.[14] We go from mechanical and dynamic schemes to extreme personalization, based on history or behavior, with the risks of crafting propositions that are impossible to pass on, especially for shoppers who are fast with credit cards.[15]

Once again, toilet paper doesn't need a digital twin and an inverted supply chain. At least, not as urgently as strategic industries, like mobility, energy, luxury, hospitality, and so forth. A flipped supply (digital first, physical later) is the best fit for brand VIPs, even in a world without blockchain at first. The question for the brand managers of the future is: whom should I engage to make my product innovation successful?[16] Who should I talk to to get relevant feedback for my network of employees and suppliers? What is the price for that in-market insight and push?

Tech makes us think of the price as a function of the willingness of a VIP to play with the brand, first digitally and then in the physical world. People will wait to pick up the branded merchandise, physically, only when the price is right. Will the world look and behave like a big, fat gaming arena? Let's see. For sure, it will no longer be necessary to ask a salesperson, "How much is it?" In the future, there will be no salespeople and no stores: yes, let me exaggerate a bit, to make sure this point cuts through.

2.5. We, a People of Traders

Whether you are selling chocolate or dental insurance, the big conundrum to solve, every single year, is the sell-in, that is, the purchasing plan of distributors or wholesale chains, and of direct channels, and their commitment towards forecast gaps and unsold items. Today's companies have an imperative to sell more units, ideally many more than last year, if they want to enjoy a quiet Christmas dinner. They usually share a piece of the margins with the distribution network, both online and offline, to maximize visibility via periodic in-store programs, as physical, digital and mental availability is key for

---

[14] One example is software solutions like Nibble. See: www.nibbletechnology.com. What's interesting, and scary, is - and we quote from their website: "Nibble is built by a team of academically trained experts in negotiation, behavioral science and conversational design focused on delivering win-win outcomes at scale." AI is a great negotiator and may trick people into offers they can't refuse. Legislation may need to evolve, to protect the weak and unaware from the risks of moving from personalization to addiction.

[15] Obviously, under-age shoppers, older audiences and psychologically weak fans need to be protected from machines, whose code may be programmed to solely maximize sales.

[16] The best use case of this new idea of engagement and compensation of co-creators is Nike's Swoosh platform. For more information, see: www.swoosh.nike.

the success of any annual contract with shareholders.[17] Sales promotions are of great help when numbers need to be made quickly, at each month and year-end closing.

Now, by flipping this linear flow, which goes from manufacturing to distribution, to the final users, technology ends up killing the middleman. New product releases, as mentioned, can be dropped into fans' wallets directly, in a digital format, while manufacturing and shipping will happen on demand, and through a fractional universe of intermediaries offering 3D printing, warehousing, rental, delivery and pickup services, all of it with ad hoc costs or subscription services.

One of the things that traditional retailers or distribution chains do well is the branded experience. There are tons of articles about in-store and omni-channel theater. Walking down Oxford Street in London is rewarding as an experience, in addition to the satisfaction of a shopping craving, exposed and discussed via the classic in-store ritual with a store associate. If that experience completely shifts to the digital terrain, which precedes any physical interaction or purchase, what remains of brick-and-mortar shops is a physical infrastructure that needs to flirt with fans, to get them what they need, if they need it, and only on demand. Brands and distribution used to be a commercial cartel, extracting value from people. Fans are now in the driver's seat, with distribution and tech stacks waiting for their signal to deliver to them, in just ten minutes, the magic they have been waiting for. It is the time of the fan as the true business emperor. Retail starts to think more like a media or an entertainer.

Again, we don't mean to burn down shopping malls, figuratively. Distribution must stop thinking that its supreme mission is just to sell, or to pass ownership of an object from the warehouse to a stranger. That game is over. Having the same message across multiple touchpoints won't do the magic. The big shift is to talk less and understand and predict more. We need lots of data and the right tech to capture it.

2.6. The Person at the Center

The Mad Men had one mission: land on people's shopping lists, which exponentially improves the chances of a purchase. Whatever happened after the purchase was relegated to minor departments, like customer care. In the golden age of marketing, this was labeled 'brand love', which is more like a date and dump two-step dance or a one-night stand, to be more precise.

---

[17] We refer here to main findings from: Byron Sharp, *How Brands Grow: What Marketers Don't Know*, Oxford University Press, 2010.

Everything is different in the days of exponential technologies. Blockchain and AI create a holy alliance between brands and superfans, and the latter now have every interest in spreading the brand's word. The rewards can be immense, if we think of perks and benefits shared in full security and floating at high multiples of the initial release price, thanks to controlled secondary markets.[18] Marketing is no longer a one-sided lesson or an arrow pointing at people's hearts. Fans' minds and wallets win over love.

Marketing is now a secure and private relationship among creators of value, no matter which side they are on, be it the brand corner or the fan bench. The digital format of every good will be created first, and disseminated through communities, which will become the real marketing department, both for innovation and communication, capturing that 10 to 15 percent of net sales that is today dedicated to the fourth P of the marketing mix, namely the classic communication programs. It does not take an entire village to grow a brand. It just takes two sides: brand and fans.

What's new? Technology can accurately track all brand/fan/fan transactions, thus creating the highways where the most creative brand/consumer duos will thrive, for eternity, as blockchains will never stop recording the success of a great idea.

One example of this unbreakable - let's give it this name – 'proof of community inclusion' comes from Mina Protocol, a popular layer-one blockchain[19], which was designed to protect critical information about each fan, thanks to what the experts call "zero knowledge proof" (ZKP) while allowing computing power to remain lightweight (under 22 KB.) Mina allows fast and easy verifiable identities, without the need to release unnecessary information, powering a new type of engagement and exchange fan-to-fan, without the friction of verifying identities and histories of each stakeholder at each transaction. This type of set-up is perfect for cross-partnerships, where brands can leverage in full and monetize their user base, without giving away fans' details. The value unlocked, at max speed and security, is unprecedented.[20]

Every marketer's dream finally comes true.

---

[18] The most compelling case is the proceeds from Nike's NFTs in 2021, as recorded by Dune Analytics, a research institution - www.dune.com. The company made $185 Mil, while its fans made cumulatively $1.3 Bil from secondary transactions.

[19] To know more about the Mina Protocol, visit: https://minaprotocol.com/.

[20] Zero Knowledge Proof, or ZKP, is just a methodology to prove a fact or a statement, without having to see the underlying data, which is usually not registered on chain, thus freeing up space and energy, and making the whole blockchain more effective and energy efficient. Mina operations can, therefore, be run from smaller devices vs. the usual processing units of the first generation blockchains, like Ethereum.

We need to solve for a smoother consumer journey, remove fears and speculations around the blockchain world, and strive for clarity in terms of regulations. But this is going to happen, and the world will look very different a few years from now. Transactions will be safe, fast, and transparent, forever, says Kurt Hemecker, former CEO at Mina[21].

The Mad Men can finally leave an eternal mark on the world. But they owe it to the real brand managers: their users. The goal of brands is not to tell people what to place on their shopping list, as mentioned earlier, but to ask the super-influencers if they can join a brand's list of family and friends.[22] The balance of power has shifted in favor of the fan.

Let consumers help you understand and finesse what you can do for them. Use tech, make sense of the data, and find patterns in what's going on in your database. If there is something you don't know or need to verify, talk to your fans, feature them, celebrate them. Let them run your show. For example, you are a DTC airline, and they use you to fly to London to shop? Make sure you get them there on time. And, if they allow you, be on their side, to make their experience unique and memorable, serving them a glass of French champagne at the VIP lounge, as they wait to go back home after an epic weekend. Hire the brand's true owners: the big spenders, the loud and proud evangelists, the smart socialites, the brainy and fun creators, the honeymooners, the family planning heroes, the fair feed-backers, and the sick *consiglieres*. You are the concierge of someone else's owner suite[23].

You are going to be surprised. Fans are ready to help you if you let them. Both sides, consumer and manufacturer, have the same incentives in increasing their own interest, brag about how smart they are in their choices, and work for a cumulated higher social capital. Karl Marx might be proud of that, perhaps. We did not kill *Das Kapital*.[24] We have decentralized it and made it accurate and intelligent, thanks to blockchain and AI.

---

[21] Hemecker, Kurt, Former CEO at the Mina Foundation. Interview with Frank Pagano. 09/05/2024. Zurich.

[22] The Nike 2021 NFTs example is led by a small group of super-fans. It's enough to recruit your best VIPs to make a marketing program succeed.

[23] A quick ride through Instagram and Tik Tok, especially looking at beauty craft brands, will show how upcoming brands celebrate their users and feature them, as if they were in charge. And they are. For example, see: www.refybeauty.com. Technology is an enabler of a new marketing approach. Technology allows brands to connect at scale and at zero cost with their ultimate 'brand managers,' namely their best fans and users.

[24] *Das Kapital* is Karl Marx's most famous opera (1867) and the bible of the Communist movement.

2.7. Back to the Future

Exponential technologies hit the marketing mix right in its chest. The funnel, the path of interaction between brand and consumer, is now reversed. It is a loop, where everything is digital and contains intangible elements, such as ideas, rights, and options. Brand equity becomes liquid and decentralized, and must be managed through continuous exchanges, where creators and brands trade data and interact, to increase the value of their services, beyond what takes place in the physical world. Old world brand managers, distribution, and media have lost their war, or at least their rent positions. Exchanges across all actors will be fast and efficient. Everything is executed privately and securely. Most importantly, you will not start the funnel by saying: "tell me about yourself, dear brand, so I can buy you." The new mantra is: "give me everything that you have digitally and right away, because 'I' am your distributor, seller and buyer, when I decide, and here is my history and data." The marketing funnel must be reversed if it is to survive.

The 4 Ps will give way to two new heroes: (1) the meta-product; (2) the independent self, who sets prices, distributes and does marketing for the brand, for their own tangible interest and not for love. It's like a talking product, which interacts with a talking fan, with their dialogue powered by technology.

Tech will reward us all for everything we do, and for the data that we can feed back or share, for any brand out there. It will make us less romantic, more efficient, less inclined to ownership, and above all, more rational when it comes to production and consumption. After all, it is not a bad world to live in when marketing is decentralized, and technology helps capable people, creators, ambassadors and good marketers, among the fan base, to succeed, just as companies and brands have always done in the past.

We have outlined a future that tastes very much of science fiction, but which, in our view, is likely to start taking place within five years from now. We repeat: this is not happening tomorrow morning. At this point, a fair business question might be: What can I do immediately? The answer, again, is to start progressively changing the 4 Ps, with small steps.

The moral of the story is not that we will drastically reduce mass production and physical presence. This will happen in rare cases, like luxury and the world of services, healthcare or education, just to name a few. The immediate lesson that we can draw is:

- Start delivering products and services with certified supply chains and unique brand experiences.

- Break the mold of standardized pricing, contemplating ongoing VIP discounts, personalized value for money and value for action and data, kickbacks and incentives, while accurately tracking participation and engagement.

- Open the menu of trading options, from selling to renting, from reusing to recycling, while leveraging after-sale interactions, as if they were primary media.

- Federate with the brand's best consumers and partners, to enlist them in a journey of co-creation and co-narration, paying them fairly.[25]

Let technology handle the bulk of these data flows and processes, while the Mad Men can finally devote themselves to what every company should be doing, all the time: Increase the social capital of fans and the well-being of the communities in which they operate, from employees to suppliers, from neighbors to the local networks they inhabit.

As mentioned at the beginning of the chapter, the straight line that goes from production to shipments, from sales to customer service, benefited mostly manufacturers and distributors, who outsourced most of the externalities and extracted value from fans. The brand power commands a premium to be paid, which includes healthy margins, which, today, are distributed unevenly across the food chain.

---

[25] Does people's data have value, and how much is it worth? The large fines inflicted by the EU authorities to big tech (for example, Alphabet, Meta, Tik Tok) highlight, if anything, that there is tremendous value associated with data. For a Top 10 GDPR fines' list, see: *The 10 largest GDPR fines on Big Tech*, TechCrunch, August 2024. There are many ways to calculate the cost per action, digitally and physically. One metric could be the Cost Per Thousand (CPM,) which is the cost of reaching 1,000 users on Facebook, for example, which is approximately $9-10 in 2024. There are many other pricing schemes. In summary, data is money, and making sense of it is the new oil, or gold. We hope that this book is read by some quantitative economist, who is willing to build a different model around data markets, or at least one that is alternative to the current one, where platforms' owners extract most rewards.

The only benchmark that we could find in this respect is Web3 gaming. Yat Siu, Founder and Chairman at Animoca Brands, a fund and one of the best Web3 platforms, states: "Web3 gaming (...) offers better chances to secure paying users, to have a healthier and faster path to financial sustainability, and to protect IP. Unlike traditional games, blockchain-based games can be profitable with just a few thousand users, while having richer content and diversity and higher engagement, thanks to a fairer distribution of resources across the ecosystem (participants receive rewards and benefits commensurate with their efforts.) Capitalism is an economic system that promotes change and is disruptive by nature because it is based on market competition, favoring entities that are better able to compete. Innovation means change. Stability is a feature of closed oligopolistic markets," (*The future of gaming: An interview with Yat Siu, Chairman of the Board, Animoca Brands*, The Cryptonomist, February 2024.)

What if data, with the right incentives, could help to boost everyone's interests, while making this whole process less resource-intensive and exhausting for the planet? What if sustainability gets baked into Total Marketing? What if the data produced by the full network of suppliers, manufacturers, employees, distributors and users is so powerful to curve that straight line into a circle, where information is flowing, and rewards are proportionally shared across all parties involved? What if there were a better way of running our most strategic industries?

2.8. Healthy Meta-Products

With that thought in mind, we decided to speak to Enrico Perfler, Founder at 1 MED[26], a company born in 2014 and based in Switzerland. Perfler is a serial entrepreneur and a former university professor, who decided to create a different Contract Research Organization (CRO), with a focus on medical devices and now pharmaceuticals. His approach wants to be proactive, and it is based on deep tech and a world-class knowledge of global regulations across the EU and the US. 1 MED is a SME[27], with 150 employees, double-digit growth in yearly revenues and it is focused on innovation for big pharma and health-tech scaleups. According to its Founder, its goal is to make pharma supply chains more efficient.

The usual innovation ritual, if we think of a standard medical device, is to start with clinical studies, and then move on to a long protocol of small and larger tests on humans, before getting EU or FDA[28] (US) approval, followed by launch and large-scale production.

The initial investment is massive. Once clearance is given to a specific medical device, the go-to-market machine needs to scale fast to deliver the return on investment that all stakeholders expect. Feedback on the product per se is usually collected through questionnaires, with scarce incentives and low redemption rates. Risks are higher for B2C propositions, and crises are always handled ex-post, with the usual long tail of legal proceedings and risk of class actions coming back to haunt manufacturers. Perfler confirms: "we don't have a continuous loop of real-life evidence of how our products are being used in the real world. That would be essential to help us improve what we do, minimizing risks on all sides, from the manufacturer to the final users[29]."

---

[26] You can find more information on www.1med.ch.

[27] Small - Medium Enterprise; Enrico Perfler prefers that definition to start-up or scale-up.

[28] It's the US Food and Drugs Administration, a federal bureau, which approves all new drugs and devices on US territory.

[29] Perfler, Enrico, Founder at 1 MED. Interview with Frank Pagano. 08/21/2024. Zurich.

New news is that 1 MED is working, together with strategic partners, like Circular Protocol[30], a fourth-generation layer-one blockchain, which also uses AI under its hood, on a system that will collect data in hospitals, to get field data linked to its devices. The aim is to have all data about the tools, the physicians, the practitioners, and the patients. Data, both from the good doctors and the bad ones, is key, or from the top guns and the cargo pilots, to use a metaphor. Enough and varied evidence should help any CRO research, understand faster, and act accordingly. All medical records are already digitized. AI can sift through the data, previously anonymized, and help understand what doesn't work and how tools, devices and pharmaceuticals can be improved, or if there are other factors driving deviations from plans or projections, like human mistakes.

Perfler concludes: "smart contracts, done on blockchain, can redistribute the rewards across employees of medical organizations and patients, as health care organizations would be willing to pay for that chest of gold data[31]."

This is something that is already within reach, as Anima Anandkumar, Professor at Caltech and former AI Scientist at tech giant Nvidia, shows in her work. By using AI, manufacturers of medical gear can extract meaning and insight from usage data, with the goal of designing anti-infection catheters, which makes the manufacturers more trustworthy, their products better, their returns lower, their customer care more effective, and so forth.[32] It's happening.

The importance of streamlining the collection and refinery of medical data for better R&D and innovation, with the goal of having a more efficient, effective and personalized medicine is also at the heart of a couple of test cases led by the Life Sciences Cluster Basel, Switzerland, which show exactly the benefits of a data based approach for the full chain that goes from patients to manufacturers, passing through hospitals and practitioners. Health data should be collected in such a way that it can be used both in healthcare delivery and in research and development (by industry and academia) while considering all legal, ethical, and economic frameworks. This will lead to the creation of services and products that can be marketed and that help people with their health prevention and care. Currently, data must be provided again and again to hospitals and institutions, as it is not captured and utilized in a standardized structure.

---

[30] For more information, see www.circularlabs.io/home. The author is a minority shareholder at Circular.

[31] Perfler, Enrico, Founder at 1 MED. Interview with Frank Pagano. 08/21/2024. Zurich.

[32] The paper was published in the scientific journal Science Advances, with the title *AI-aided geometric design of anti-infection catheters*, January 2024, Vol. 10, Issue 1.

A broadly supported, common strategy is lacking. A shift in thinking is slowly taking place. Without data there is no healthcare and no public health. And sharing data helps the healing process. In the complexity of healthcare, collaboration is not an option, but a necessity, says Philippe Hofstetter[33], Project Manager at the Life Science Cluster Basel.[34]

Sharing data becomes so vital for the future of healthcare that the scenario of not sharing it publicly could represent a burden and stifle innovation.[35] Would regional industrial champions like that? Would governments allow it? There is plenty of evidence that acting is the way to go.

In this vision, everyone has the tangible, monetary incentive to comply. Blockchain would guarantee privacy and transparency, while AI would make sense of the numbers and proactively generate recommendations for action, in fractions of a second. Ownership of the data would sit with hospitals or laboratories, and a piece of the pie would go to employees and patients, as well. As shown above, we have inverted the funnel, and the innovation process starts from the jungle, from the network, using tools and devices. Innovation would always start with hard facts and market evidence, making the testing phase more efficient and informed. The person is at the center of the whole equation.

The true advantage of 1 MED, to go back to the initial example of this section, is their expertise and brand, as much as the strength of the network of available

---

[33] Hofstetter, Philippe, Project Manager at the Life Science Cluster Basel. Interview with Frank Pagano. 09/20/2024. Zurich.

[34] For more information, see: www.lifesciencesbasel.com. The organization also collaborates with research and university institutions, like the University of Basel - WWZ. The pioneering project BâleDat, initiated by the Life Sciences Cluster Basel, of the Chamber of Commerce of both Basels, is a bottom-up approach from the region. BâleDat aims to advance the secondary use of structured, anonymized, and standardized health data in collaboration with all regional stakeholders and in cooperation with top-down projects such as DigiSanté and the Swiss Personalized Health Network (SPHN). "Hospitals from both Basels, the pharmaceutical industry, business associations, and the SPHN are jointly seeking cross-cantonal solutions, based on jointly identified use cases. Thanks to BâleDat, a shift in thinking has already taken place among many stakeholders in our region. Additionally, DigiSanté is a promising federal program that we want to support from the region," says Hofstetter.

[35] For example, extremely interesting is a paper from 2024, from WWZ itself: Riccardo Bentele and Rolf Weder, *On the Importance of Swiss Patient Data for Pharmaceutical R&D in Switzerland*, University of Basel - WWZ, April 2024. Quoting from the abstract: "Real-world data (RWD) are an increasingly important input into the pharmaceutical R&D process as shown by countries like the USA or Finland. As the availability of and access to Swiss RWD is rather limited, the question arises whether this creates a burden for pharmaceutical R&D in Switzerland."

data and stakeholders; all parties would have a vested interest in increasing their mutual social capital. Healthcare needs devices that go beyond their mere function, be it collecting humans' fluids, for example ('meta' in 'meta-product' is, indeed, Greek for 'beyond'), plus it requires a healthy dose of tech and data. 1 MED and Enrico Perfler, its Founder, are already working on it.

2.9. SupplAI for Smart Products

The data around how we manufacture our products will be key, if you ask Silviu Homoceanu, Ph.D., co-founder and CTO at Deltia [36], a scaleup of approximately 20 people, born in November 2022 inside the Merantix campus in Berlin, one of the world's best hubs for AI.[37] Homoceanu and his team already have clients, like ABB and Viessmann, and their first products are breaking ground. Like all scaleups, their roadmap is extremely crowded, and it's based on hardware-enabled software solutions, which build on proprietary AI models. Their focus is on the big industrial supply chains.

Thanks to AI, factories can eliminate waste and optimize their processes. AI allows you to manage production lines in a more proactive fashion.

> We install optical sensors along the lines and continuously extract information about everything that happens, monitoring throughput against set production plans, for example, or even predicting impact on the employees' well-being, just by looking at ergonomic data of their movements. The system works also for manual operations. Privacy is respected by design in our software solutions, affirms Homoceanu[38].

Benefits are real. ABB is reportedly improving productivity by 15% on the products where Deltia's solutions are in use. There is the additional benefit of stabilizing and better controlling production, especially thinking about shocks coming from external factors, like the ones we saw during the COVID-19 era.

The future is one where strategic information about the functioning of a production line can help manufacturers with their workforce, with product innovation, and with supplier management. The future is one where technology will shape smarter factories, animate more intelligent robots along production lines and provide simulation systems for scenario analyses (via

---

[36] Find all information regarding Deltia at www.deltia.ai.

[37] Merantix, based in Berlin, is a fund, a portfolio of companies and a campus, and it's believed to be the most important AI hub in Europe. For more information: www.merantix.com.

[38] Homoceanu, Silviu, Co-founder and CTO at Deltia. Interview with Frank Pagano. 08/21/2024. Zurich.

digital twins of lines or factories, for example), improving quality and efficiency to the maximum.

The next step will be to have sensors on products, like ABB's turbines, and not only inside factories. That data will help manufacturers make sense of product performance in real life. Supply is destined to observe demand closely and continuously, and to meet it faster, all thanks to data. "That is something that we have in our pipeline, so product usage data is on its way," reassures Homoceanu[39]. This is another confirmation of the advent of meta-factories and meta-products, which will talk to all stakeholders in the real world and feedback essential data on how to manufacture future products, for a progressively better and smarter world.

2.10. Will You Marry Me in Sorrento? A Meta-Website Called Nina

Nina is the AI-powered avatar and chatbot, which was introduced in 2022 by the small town of Sorrento, in the divine Amalfi Coast (Italy), on the municipal website, as the helper and concierge for all official and mundane information related to one of the most sought-after destinations, especially by American tourists. Elvis Presley himself made an English rendition of a famous Neapolitan song, called *Torna a Surriento* (literally 'come back to Sorrento,' which became *Surrender* in Presley's recording). So, the destination is known to the rich and romantic global elite.

Nina works 24/7, speaks multiple languages and uses AI to serve, instantly, a personalized consumer journey to all users out there. Would you like to organize your wedding in Sorrento, from official documentation to suggestions for hotels, restaurants, and things to see for your in-laws? Consider it done! Would you like to mint all official documents and your own vows on Cardano[40], receiving an eternal token right in your Inbox[41]? Easy! Nina is the creation of QuestIT, which together with The Digital Box, is a digital group whose Founder and President is Marco Landi, COO and President of Apple Computer Inc. between 1994-1997[42].

---

[39] Ibid.

[40] Cardano is one of the most important blockchains in the world. Its founder was a Co-founder and the only CEO of Ethereum, the most popular blockchain after Bitcoin. For more information, see www.cardanofoundation.org.

[41] This is a feature created by a company called Tokenance, based in Lugano, and called RE-TWIN. More information on: www.tokenance.io. The author is a minority shareholder at Tokenance.

[42] Steve Jobs would return to Apple in 1997. So, Mr. Landi was the company's top executive, before Jobs would make his return to the company he founded.

The addition of exponential technologies to a simple website boosts the potential of a small village and allows a community with little means to cater an ultra-personalized service to international clients, at scale and with world-class quality, at a cost that remains manageable for local public budgets. Tech becomes the secret helper of local employees, who would not have the chance to act and react at the level of an AI-powered tool, let alone handle multiple language skills. The flow of information and orders being generated via Nina builds a network of suppliers, from hotels to tour guides, from chauffeurs to restaurants, from local offices and religious institutions to multiple touch points, to upsell and cross-sell customers with offerings that are well-suited for their needs.

The magic is the ability to use, in no time, an exponential technology, without disrupting the current tech stack (a simple website) and dramatically helping employees and suppliers to play a world-class game, without having to wait for a full cultural transformation of the public administration to happen. Brands may even consider joining the party and pay for that gold list of global and rich tourists, thus creating incremental cash flows into the public treasury (of course, in line with GDPR).

It's all about data and making sense of the data, once exponential tech is in place. George Clooney and Amal Alamuddin, Kim Kardashian and Kanye West, Tom Cruise and Katie Holmes, for example, all got married on the Amalfi Coast. Maybe you don't have the same wedding planner as these superstars, but would you like to have a go and just get a sense of what and how it could be? Just ask Nina. Welcome to your new meta-site, a talking product and service.

No place on earth is too foreign, and it's only one click away. Sorrento becomes a product, or a small city, you can talk to, and a network of employees and suppliers at your service, which you can access via the filter of what's locally relevant and of your needs, courtesy of AI. Can you resist the beauty of a talking town? All you need to do is *Surrender*.[43]

2.11. Milk it: The Business of Engaging Suppliers

Christian Peter Mueller is the Head of Dairy Sourcing and Sales, besides leading the agenda for the Environmental Sustainability Affairs in Switzerland for the world's number one food producer, Nestlé. His job is to lead the dairy business

---

[43] You may think of this example as a 'platform' economy or case, to use a famous marketing theory, or at least slang. It's for sure interesting how a simple town can function as a network of service and product providers. Our point here is on the augmentation of this network, already existing, thanks to data capture and data refinery. If Sorrento is a platform – and we are fine with that – AI and blockchain would make it an augmented platform.

in Switzerland, nurturing the relationships with the local farmers and buying fresh milk, which is used for Nestlé's infant formula product line.

"We use the protein part of the milk, and we sell part of the fat, which can be used to make cream, for example," says Mueller[44]. But that's not the whole story. Mueller is also overseeing external relations, like the ones with government, trade associations and research institutions, which can help him transform the dairy business. On top, and this is a counterintuitive addition, there is the whole sustainability component, namely the leadership of Nestlé's sustainability projects across categories in Switzerland, where dairy is key.[45] What does purchasing milk at scale have to do with the greenhouse gas emissions of its network? Why talk to universities or local authorities, and bother with the big picture?

> We have the objective to reduce emissions in dairy by 20% in 6 years. We need the whole supply chain, if we want to win. This is why we reached out to Emmi (a supplier and a buyer of ours, as well as a competitor) and we started engaging farmers and the public as well. We want impact and we need to work together with the industry, to change it, says Mueller[46].

The Swiss Federation and the Department of Agriculture have disbursed money into the project, as it has an obvious social importance. Agriculture represents 15% of the total greenhouse gas emissions in Switzerland[47], so the government has a vested interest in partnering with private businesses, and Nestlé is the leader in dairy. On the other hand, over 70% of Nestle's emissions are Scope 3[48], and about half of that part is dairy, so the company has a reason to act with the key stakeholders in the field, if it wants to reach its targets. The only way to make this work sits outside of the four walls of each and every player. We need everyone at the table.

---

[44] Mueller, Peter Christian, Head of Dairy Sourcing and Sales Nestlé Switzerland. Interview with Frank Pagano. 09/06/2024. Zurich.

[45] For more information, see: www.klimastar-milch.ch.

[46] Mueller, Peter Christian, Head of Dairy Sourcing and Sales Nestlé Switzerland. Interview with Frank Pagano. 09/06/2024. Zurich.

[47] For all stats about the Nestle roadmap to Net Zero, see: https://www.nestle.com/sustainability/climate-change/zero-environmental-impact. For more information about Switzerland, see: https://www.agroscope.admin.ch/agroscope/en/home/topics/livestock/ruminants/ammonia-reduction-in--cattle-husbandry/facts-figures.html.

[48] In simplified terms, Scope 1 emissions are directly emitted by a company; Scope 2 are indirect emissions from a company's purchased energy; Scope 3 are indirect emissions from its upstream and downstream value chain. For more information, see the EU Commission website: www.commission.europa.eu.

But what's needed is also accurate data. Nestlé built a baseline for all farms. They measured the status quo, took the average of three years of greenhouse emissions, so that they could hedge against unusual variations (2019 - 21) and worked with a team from the Department of Applied Sciences from the University of Bern.[49] Together with their scientists, the team created their own greenhouse gas evaluation tool to measure footprint and performance.

"We wanted precision and perfect fit with our objectives. We took the time to do it right," explains Mueller[50].

Once the baseline is set, farmers are trained, assisted and immersed in a plan to boost their productivity, while managing overall emissions. It's a balancing act between throughput and a lower footprint. You can't go fast and just maximize one. You need balance.

> Each year we measure where the farmers are. If results are in line with the plan, the farmers get a reward, calibrated to their individual situation. The incentive may arrive at between CHF 5 to 10 cents per kilo of milk, which is a solid kick[51]. Of course there is a spread: some farmers get zero, as not everyone complies, and some need to do more, but at least 80% of the farmers have taken some measures towards a better management of the soil and the cattle, reassures Mueller[52].

It's a fine balance, as mentioned, because productivity gains per cow are easiest to realize, for example, by feeding more energy to the cows (more corn), but that could lead to higher consumption of ingredients and therefore clash with the project's second objective: the feed-food competition. Balance is needed for a long-term sustainability impact.

This is a clear case of engagement of suppliers, partners, public authorities and research institutions, and even competitors, right from the source (the fields) to create efficiency and quality, while benefiting the whole value chain. Procurement used to be all about pricing, especially at big corporations like Nestlé, where cents multiplied by the large orders have an immediate impact on the P&L. The approach is different in this case. It starts from the broad context,

---

[49] For more information, see: www.bfh.ch.

[50] Mueller, Peter Christian, Head of Dairy Sourcing and Sales Nestlé Switzerland. Interview with Frank Pagano. 09/06/2024. Zurich.

[51] The official Swiss reference price is approximately CHF 80 cents per kilo. For more information, see: https://www.ip-lait.ch/richtpreise-2024/.

[52] Mueller, Peter Christian, Head of Dairy Sourcing and Sales Nestlé Switzerland. Interview with Frank Pagano. 09/06/2024. Zurich.

and the dialogue with suppliers also includes knowledge sharing, incentives, and common targets, so that the whole nation can thrive in the future.

They have one annual workshop with all stakeholders, to discuss tools and incentives, but especially to transparently share plans and progress. It's almost like a movement. It's money back to farmers and cultural change. They created a shared feeling and mission to drive impact on the entire country, or at least the whole industry. This is data-driven, social change in action.

The data is true gold for public institutions and universities. And the model could be applied to non-Nestlé farmers, too, when potentially scaling up the project to the whole market, at the end of the six years of the current phase. In the future, data could potentially be monetized also for entities interested in risk assessment, real estate development or the voluntary markets for carbon credits, unlocking incremental resources. The model could be white-labeled and sold to other regions and companies. There are more and more pockets of value that could be unlocked if more monetary resources were needed.

What Mueller started is the beginning of a comprehensive path, where the engagement of the farmers rhymes with sustainability and a fair and transparent procurement scheme. Sustainability becomes a part of the marketing mix, thanks to data collected across the network. Sustainability is baked into a tech-augmented business.

The project is being used for internal and external communication, having an impact on Nestlé's reputation and retention of talents, and with fans and trade. The network of suppliers, which is usually fungible (and assessed through the prism of just 'the lower price wins'), becomes a platform to make employer branding and to feature in the dialogue with fans and retailers. The Swiss quality is a key differentiator, and fans want the best for their kids. What's starting here is a revolution for the whole industry, leveraging assets that are usually undervalued, like farmers and their data.

In 2020 Nestlé set targets for net-zero by 2050, but the dairy team had already experimented with some tests before that decision. The execution has been, so far, orchestrated by a team of internal entrepreneurs and open-minded managers, who rallied the whole network around the business, with the objective to change the face of the industry and of the country. Companies don't just buy milk cheap to serve great infant formulas at a profit, like in the old days. The brands and managers of the future collect data and inspire the whole network behind a bigger dream, a long-term plan made of a Total Marketing vision. Running a business no longer means that you just milk it.

2.12. Twinning Supply

Virginie Maillard works for Siemens, one of the largest industrial companies on the planet, where she leads the global research for the Simulation and Digital Twin Technology[53], from her office in New Jersey (US), while also carrying the responsibility for key markets, like Germany, India and China. Before Siemens, she worked in the automotive industry, which is being taken by storm by multiple revolutions, starting from electrification. She is probably the best person to talk to about supply chain disruption and the trend of "twinning" what we manufacture, or the factories *per se*, where everything gets created in the first place.

A digital twin is a digital representation of real machines and factories, buildings and cities, networks and transport systems, which evolves with their lifecycle. As a digital prototype, it helps to define and optimize the product and production system, before investing in physical assets. This reduces the need for physical, more resource intensive, prototypes. Later, it helps monitor and optimize the operation of the real systems by testing changes in a digital environment before implementing them in the real world, says Maillard[54], confirming our description of a flipped supply chain, where digital always precedes physical.

The efficiencies of a set-up based on twins are massive, for the full network of stakeholders revolving around whatever value chain, with the added benefit of delivering the best outcome for the final customer.

The digital twin generates tremendous value by running 'what if' scenarios and predicting future performance and behavior. It lays the foundation for making quick and confident decisions before acting in the real world. It also helps to reduce time to market and ensures that specific requirements are met. Users get direct feedback on their actions – when they change settings or create new scenarios, they experience the impact and can make better and confident decisions. Data suddenly becomes understandable and tangible, leading to more reliable decision-making. The digital twin is the practical solution for mastering industry's challenges: reducing CO_2 footprint, improving sustainability, increasing resilience, and speeding up processes and time to market. It looks like there will not be another way of running a business in the future; it needs, however, reliable data underneath and computing power to

---

[53] For more information, see: www.siemens.com.

[54] Maillard, Virginie, Head of Technology US and of Simulation & Digital Twin Research at Siemens. Interview with Frank Pagano. 08/29/2024. Zurich.

perform iterative scenario analyses, especially when the stakes are high or when we use taxpayers' money for huge infrastructural investments.

Good news is the twins are not identical, and the digital one is poised to be smarter and smarter, leading the way before its physical alter ego.

> In the future, the digital twin will become increasingly interactive and immersive. At Siemens we call this the Industrial Metaverse: an immersive environment, potentially with photo-realistic visualization, which allows a multitude of users to easily interact with digital twins. It will be a new and powerful collaboration tool for engineering and manufacturing operations, Maillard closes[55].

Technology, as we saw, becomes the enabler of multi-stakeholder and enhanced collaboration, in smart and immersive environments, helped by tech stacks like AI and blockchains, or virtual and augmented reality. This is another confirmation of the shift from simple products to meta-products, and from supply chains to open ecosystems, based on data syndication and multimodal interfaces. We can create a better future, and we can even test it beforehand. Listening to Ms. Maillard, one thing is sure: We can twin and test the supply.

2.13. Twinning Luxury

The idea of a digital twin (or passport) fits very well with scarcity. As humans, we have always admired the fine craft of a *maestro*, like a watchmaker, a jeweler and a leather artisan, let alone the creative hand of a *couturier*. And yet, gray and counterfeit products infest our marketplaces, with no elasticity to global crises or shocks. Plus, we don't really know where all the components of an accessory are sourced, and if that happens ethically. If we are buying something unique, can we get access to its supply chain and receive firm confirmation of compliance and excellence, as a default feature for what is probably the purchase of a lifetime, like an engagement ring? It's time technology came to the rescue, to save artists, as well as consumers, chasing their dream of exclusivity. This is why we speak to Romain Carrere, CEO at the Aura Blockchain Consortium [56] (or, more simply, Aura,) a blockchain and non-profit organization, whose daily focus is the protection of over forty luxury *maisons*, including groups like LVMH, Prada Group, Only The Brave (OTB Group), and many more. By caring about craftsmanship, they also care about the community

---

[55] Ibid.

[56] For more information, see: www.auraconsortium.com.

of lovers around it. Aura's main offerings are Digital Product Passports (DPP) and digital collectibles, in the form of NFTs.

He studied finance in London and Boston, but has always been a geek at heart and started coding when he was a kid. After the events of 9/11, Carrere left the US and went back to Europe to become a tech entrepreneur and serial start-up founder. Web3 and blockchain have always intrigued him, so when the job opportunity at Aura came up, it felt like it was destiny.

Aura wants to set a new standard for the luxury industry. They support groups like LVMH, Prada Group, OTB Group, as well as many independent luxury brands, in their digitization and Customer Experience journey. It's 40 brands for now, and 40 million products already registered on our blockchain. The so-called Digital Product Passport regulation will come into effect in 2027, so the group is helping brands get ready for the consumer of the future, who will want transparency and benefits via their DPP for each of their luxury purchases.

Aura is a consortium, so all new brands need to be approved by its board, made up of all current partners. They decided to work only with luxury propositions and govern an agnostic set of blockchain solutions, offering the advantages of private and public blockchains, so that they can protect enterprise data while also giving customers Web3 utilities in full. The company provides the tech infrastructure, as well as the consulting needed to meet the needs of its members. Solutions are tailored to digital literacy and adjusted to the consumer journey to readiness, with the potential to add even more utility in the future.

There is a wide menu of options for luxury brands, from full integration into native apps to separate web apps. Also, when it comes to tracking the product, they have options from a simple QR code all the way to NFC chips, which are more evolved. For example, Rimowa inserts a chip inside the product. But the chip could also be inside a separate card, to accompany a piece of jewelry (hiding, as well, a serial number inside the jewel and the chip.) Or vision AI could be leveraged, namely a unique fingerprint on the product, like for Hublot watches, which can be scanned with a normal smartphone, while an AI-powered software analyzes the product and gives the green light of authenticity, thanks to the reading of multiple markers on the dial. Aura claims to be a one-stop shop for a complete digitization transformation.

The secondary market is a big topic, and it's on Aura's agenda, of course.

> The main objective now is traceability. Once more products will have their DPPs, we will be able to tackle the secondary markets and consumer-to-consumer trading. Transfer of ownership is feasible now,

for example towards a family member but when it comes to secondary sales, especially marketplaces, it is not widespread yet, Carrere[57] confirms.

The adoption rate and utility capabilities for any brand are progressive. Aura usually starts with a pilot, monitoring execution and KPIs. Then, there are adjustments and roll-out, according to the status and ambition of a business. It's important to bring the community with you, so communication, perks and benefits are a big part of the journey. And it's also key to educate suppliers and employees, at every touch point, as the entire supply chain can now be transparent on-chain.

A successful transition towards a blockchain-powered world requires a clear, long-term vision. Blockchain adoption is not just about complying with evolving regulations, it is also an innovative strategy to deepen consumer engagement, nurturing brand relationships. By leveraging the potential of blockchain technology in line with each stakeholder's vision, brands can ensure meaningful, successful adoption, closes Carrere[58].

Aura is launching a movement for the luxury industry, where everyone has skin in the game, and where shortcuts are no longer allowed. Twinning luxury products makes the real thing more precious than before. Meta-product features and transparent processes help a ring shine brighter and its meaning last forever, like it should be for objects that we buy to capture eternal promises of love.

2.14. What Tomorrow?

Can technology help us change the face of one of the biggest offenders of the environment, namely fashion? Can technology support us in cleaning up our act in sourcing materials for clothing and enriching our palette of business models, so that we treat better what we wear? For this reason, we speak with Vanessa Barboni Hallik, Founder & CEO at Another Tomorrow[59], a revolutionary e-commerce platform, and a community of like-minded people, for ethical fashion.

---

[57] Carrere, Romain, CEO at the Aura Blockchain Consortium. Interview with Frank Pagano. 09/05/2024. Zurich.

[58] Ibid.

[59] For more information, see: www.anothertomorrow.co.

We are modeling the future of fashion. Data and customer are at the center of the brand. The old adage was 'if you build it, they will come,' as if it was a unilateral business decision towards the market. This has changed completely. We are totally customer centric and have all key stakeholders at the heart of our vision and code of conduct. This is why knowing what our community wants is key. This is why we have a digital ID on every piece that we make, says Barboni Hallik[60].

Tracking every piece has multiple functions. First off, it's about supply chain transparency at every step of the chain. Then, a digital ID facilitates new business schemes, like repurchase, exchange of the same article, resale on the secondary market, to name just a few. So, there is a clear impact also on the consumer side. For example, let's take the size exchange program. For the evergreen products, fans can exchange a product and ask for another size, if their body has changed, for whatever reason, a pregnancy or if someone struggles to lose a few pounds. This is something that is offered for free to members. Then, there is the authentication of the product as a guarantee of its quality, or the return policy. The goal there is that the life cycle of every piece must be as long as possible, maximizing customer lifetime value at the same time. This is not perceived as a liability or an extra cost from the label's team, also because they do recruit new users via the resale market.

Another Tomorrow employs 14 people. The full transparency of processes and sourcing is a big plus in recruiting great talent, attracted by the vision and the ethos of the company, and in dealing with post-sale services. Efficiencies are generated throughout the entire value chain, and the values of the companies, lived at every step of their operations, are a driver for the low turnaround. The timeless and longevity approach to business has an impact also on design and marketing, as Another Tomorrow manufactures having multiple consumers in mind, who will love their creations, trade after trade. This is why data is essential.

Barboni Hallik also has her own approach to suppliers. Fashion can be seen, as a matter of fact, as something very similar to an agricultural product, linked to Mother Earth, unless plastic or synthetic textiles are used, if you want cheaper clothing. Most people don't realize that there is a lot in common between fashion and food. Humans grow the sources of clothing materials or extract them from animals, if you look at organic supply chains, of course. Another Tomorrow has defined a library of materials and is very strict, trusting a smaller pool of certified suppliers. For example, 98% of their wool comes from

[60] Barboni Hallik, Vanessa, Founder and CEO at Another Tomorrow. Interview with Frank Pagano. 08/31/2024. Zurich.

a single mill. There are three verticals in their strategy: environmental, human, and animal welfare. They strive to achieve best-in-class sourcing for all of them. First off, fair living wages are secured throughout the supply chain. Second, no animal sourcing. They have no conventional silk, for example. Nothing is used if that means animal suffering. Third, environmental welfare is a wide effort, which goes from processing to water usage, and extends to net zero. Manufacturing takes place in Italy. Everything is organic. Another Tomorrow has a severe protocol of audits and checks. For sure, that means its supply chain is more expensive, and decisions are made on data and hard facts.

The next item, or question, would be around money, for a business that is still mainly centered on e-commerce. You must make money in fashion, like in any other business. Being sustainable also means that you need to have a solid P&L. Another Tomorrow's EBITDA is in the low 20s. The fashion industry is based on high gross margin and large volumes, and not on risk. Fashion stakeholders and players, this is what's standard practice, accept inefficiencies on the altar of margins, knowing that they can pass the risk onto discounters and landfills.

> On the contrary, if you can reduce waste, boost inventory turns and take on more risk, using data as your ally, you could approach fashion in a different way. We took an antifragile model. We are more efficient, and we usually take on more risk in what we do. Again, technology and data are part of our mix. The biggest obstacle is the disconnect between evidence of a new trend and the time it takes to create ethical products in response. In fashion people are not willing to wait. Customer appetite means immediacy. What we are doing is to take a more timeless approach to product and design, concludes Barboni Hallik[61].

Especially for fast fashion, it is not easy to transform this industry into an environmental champion. Fans have been educated to free deliveries and returns, and to fungible and transactional relationships with their gear, pushing out responsibilities and externalities to the government and the community. Another Tomorrow is still in its early growth phase (Series A), but it's trying to set the pace for a different take on the fashion game, making its model transparent and open-sourced for all industry players.

Not much will change without regulation. Fashion is one of the most under-regulated industries in the world. Landfill in perpetuity is not sustainable. Fortunately, people are starting to treat clothing as an asset again. Disposability needs to leave space for a more expensive purchase, in the sense that business models must contemplate resale and longer life cycles, and companies must be

---

[61] Ibid.

rewarded for this ample approach to trading. Cultural attitudes can change. Sustainable and economic fashion can be achieved if we add and reward alternatives to the linear model of consumption. We need quality and data for that.

Another Tomorrow is a great example of science, discipline and vision. The hope and the model are there to create an alternative tomorrow, also for the frivolous, but so relevant fashion industry. We need fashion, as it's a part of our DNA as humans. We need it to be profitable and strong. We need it to be sustainable. This is why we must track it, end-to-end.

2.15. We, The People

Our theory holds that you can treat users as peers, and engage them in the co-creation of the content, of course, and of the very future of any enterprise. Is that real, or is it rather another romantic dream, which lives only on paper, namely on business books? Does that happen anywhere in the world and with some sort of success or traction?

This is why we decided to sit down with Sarojini, or Saro, McKenna, who is the co-founder and CEO of Dacoco, a known player and contributor to the breakthrough of the likes of Web3, NFT and the metaverse. Their most popular venture, Alien Worlds, represents one of the world's most played blockchain-based games. Alien Worlds is also one of the largest Web3 communities on the planet. So, here is a case of a community running a show, which is alive and thriving.

Dacoco was founded in 2018 as a DAO, initially in a casual and organic way.[62] Right away, it was able to generate on-chain revenues and payments, which were used to cover the costs of servers and wallets. Since the beginning, it has been community-led.

What they do is write software that allows people to co-create and exchange around a basic framework, an open canvas. In 2019, there were eight or nine other DAOs that were using their tech, and Dacoco was charging small licensing fees. It was not big enough. Gaming was a natural extension of its idea. Alien Worlds, its most famous project, is a DAO inside a gaming context. The game, per se, was the product of a side project of one of the co-founders. It has some rules and utility NFTs. Everything is built on-chain (Binance, Ethereum, and Wax) and therefore it's transparent. By the end of 2020, the

---

[62] DAO is a Decentralized Autonomous Organization, whose key decisions are made according to voting spread across the community of members, who are verified and hold the community tokens. To know more about Dacoco and Alien Worlds, see: www.dacoco.io and www.alienworlds.io.

product went live and began to develop traction. It became one of the largest games on-chain at some point, with a growing community.

What's interesting is that McKenna and her team were users and fans of the tech in the first place, and they gathered around them a group of like-minded people who wanted to build and try tools and ideas. Then, it turned into a business. This is the proof of what we would call a community-first enterprise. The network, if we want to translate this example into a business insight, is the foundation of what can potentially become an economic opportunity.

McKenna has always been driven by curiosity. With a background in business and corporate finance, she joined early blockchain and token groups and chats. Dacoco moved to Switzerland three years ago, as the crypto valley offers a friendly and clear regulatory environment. The secret lies in sharing a dream and creating space for the whole group to shape the future together.

> You need to share ownership and stakes, and you want to tangibly incentivize fans to act. In our game, you earn the internal tokens by mining, receive NFT-s, get rewards for all actions and use those tokens into the DAO for voting. For every Trillion, the name of the token, you have a vote. Once people hold skin in the game, they feel part of the company and act, beyond anyone's expectations. Within two months from the launch, fans created, for example, interfaces to read scores, did NFT drops, launched block explorers, and so forth. They became the 'brand' managers, or our marketing department. Blockchain gives everyone transparency. Tokens are liquid. On top, we gave out grants where needed. The power of the network was unleashed by sharing vision and rewards, states McKenna[63].

If people make money, the company makes money. This seems to be the economic principle behind this use case. Business models have not fully matured yet. Traditional gaming, non-blockchain-based, has the same problem. They have created a marketing audience and need to understand how to monetize it, without torturing the purity of the initial purpose and the meaning of the game.

The KPIs to assess company performance must be adjusted as well. Dacoco employs about thirty people globally, with control being progressively handed over to the community. Topline is steady, with seven million lifetime players, a few hundred thousand monthly average users (MAU) and a few thousand daily players. It would be wrong to look at this concept like you would with a

---

[63] McKenna, Sarojini, co-founder and CEO at Dacoco. Interview with Frank Pagano. 09/11/2024. Zurich.

traditional company. With Web2, we started seeing super-consumers or influencers, who helped to boost the business. These people were not engaged enough, and their endorsement was always functional and short-term focused. It was advertising, basically. With Web3, the difference is tokenization and fragmentation of ownership.

A DAO does exactly this: It gives away bigger rewards in exchange for deeper engagement. The overall economic pie turns out to be bigger. We blur the lines between fans, employees and suppliers. Of course, content doesn't need to be aesthetically beautiful, at least not always (what the geeks call triple A games), but that gives especially smaller projects space to test and scale up stuff, lowers barriers to entry, promotes innovation and reduces overproduction.

The case of Alien Worlds shows how community-led can rhyme with success, and it shows how an open system can produce wealth for all. Dacoco's point is that tech is very open. At a legal level, intellectual properties are very basic. They don't charge for the use of the brand and take more risks. Members are certified and their actions registered on the blockchain, so the digital agency is fairly compensated, differently than what goes on inside all social media platforms. It's decentralized, so the community creates content and storytelling, and votes on a bunch of content and processes. The mantra here is to build stuff that is open, or create ingredients, rather than solutions. The balance at Dacoco is to find the right dose of how much to provide; not too much and not too little.

Compensation for fans can be substantial, and some people make a living out of Alien Worlds (they are a few hundred.) It is, of course, the beginning of a path, where the community will evolve, together with the fans, always around tech and new ideas.

Speed is faster now, with exponential tech. Power to the community injects more chaos into the system. For a traditional business, this means higher risk. And, yet it's that chaos that unlocks innovation and overall value. We have been working with native web3 developers so far. The question is how to make this wide and make it fit for corporate governance and other legal requirements at enterprise level. Web3 is an interconnected system of platforms, made of simple tech tools, like a wallet, a front end, some basic rules, a community that operates the components, and lots of responsibility, but it works, confirms McKenna[64].

---

[64] Ibid.

The example of Alien Worlds tells us that we have the tech set-up to move towards a shared dream and the execution of company plans. This example demonstrates, especially, that innovation and economic value can be revamped by engaging and compensating the creators out there. Our business is made of people and for people. Tech will make rules programmable and actions tracked. Given the tall agenda that we have for our future, from sustainability to culture change, should we lose the grip on our go-to-market strategies and let the best creators in the jungle help? They will, if we let them.

2.16. We Are All in the Data Business

We are all in the data, or – better – knowledge business, no matter what we sell. This seems to be the *fil rouge* of our conversation with Simone Ungaro, who is the Chief Strategy and Innovation Officer at Leonardo[65], the Italian company that is one of the world leaders in aerospace, defense, and security.

> We make money with data, which seems an odd thing to say for someone who works for a manufacturer, for example, of planes and helicopters. The past four years have contemplated a transformation from data being a source of control and efficiency to data being an essential source of revenues. Our machines, our products, are hardware and software platforms, which are filled with sensors and continuously generating and processing data. This explodes the value of what we sell, which goes beyond a mere tool or object being transacted from us to our clients, says Ungaro[66].

The case of Leonardo, which used to be called Finmeccanica, shows very clearly how data sharing and utilization across the food chain, if leveraged and packaged as a value creator, explodes the pool of profits for all stakeholders at the table, from clients to employees to suppliers.

Their first step has been to build the infrastructure to capture, clean and access data across departments and siloes, all of that in line with laws and privacy regulations. This IT transformation was planned and rolled out over a few years. Then, AI came into play and revolutionized everything. Helicopters are being sold with value-added services, based on ten years of data, or tens and tens of terabytes of data, from over a thousand helicopters having been sold and operated, which allows them to offer apps and services that support

---

[65] For more information, see: www.leonardo.com.

[66] Ungaro, Simone, Chief Strategy and Innovation Officer at Leonardo. *Interview with Frank Pagano.* 10/18/2024. Zurich.

our clients, train future pilots, forecast maintenance, and add to products some meta-services of extreme value for clients.

"This is exactly what makes clients come back and what makes us the ideal partner for comprehensive solutions in the defense and security space, from sales to customer service, to intelligence and advisory," stresses Ungaro[67].

The software and data management innovation are as relevant as the hardware's natural improvements. The continuous strive for excellence in product and meta-product features is driven by the strict regulations and certifications needed in this industry, facilitating a swift cultural change across employees and suppliers. This is where rules can foster innovation.

> The full value chain is monitored, thanks to our systems, and in line with the latest protocols and requirements. Our suppliers are fully aware of this set-up and our employees are trained to abide. This is key if we want to retrieve information or find the root cause of potential issues or deviations from the needed standards. Our data-lake and high performing computing platform are the enablers of a world-class performance, executed by our over two thousand engineers working on our tech stack, says Ungaro[68].

Internal systems are highly secure and performing, so Ungaro doesn't see an immediate need for technologies like blockchains. AI is for sure a bigger bet for Leonardo. However, technological and digital progress sits high on Leonardo's CEO to-do list.

According to Ungaro, the CEO and the C-room are the owners of the digital and data transformation of the company. The innovation lead is like being a plumber, or – better – a builder of tubes, which make data flow across the value chain, so that every small bit of information can be turned into something of value for clients, engineers, and suppliers. Sales cycles are long and complex. It's fundamental to have the knowledge to shape the best hardware and software solutions in a very competitive industry. This is why data has become the CEO's daily bread and the first thing any company sells.

Next time you fly, just remember that a perfect machine got you there; a machine that was perfected against tons of preceding data, shared across a complex chain of manufacturers, suppliers and operators. Your next holiday, as exotic and light-hearted as it may be, will make future airplanes and vacations even more secure and enjoyable.

---

[67] Ibid.

[68] Ibid.

Future business champions will master the fine art of creating a network of extended stakeholders, where data flows seamlessly and agency is compensated fairly, and where utility is always met, from suppliers to employees to fans. We need tremendous computing power to create models that can understand, create and interact with the world. Yes, that's right, we have that. There is a new sheriff in town: Generative AI, which will augment the potential of what we discussed in the first two chapters. Making sense of what lies in front of us is even more important than measuring it. If we want sustainable, enriched products and thriving communities, we need a superior intelligence. Let's take a look at how our world will be transformed by GenAI.

Bibliography

Anandkumar, Anima, John F. Brady, Chiara Daraio, Zongyi Li, Zhiwei Peng, Paul W. Sternberg, Xuan Wan, Daniel Zhengyu Huang, Tingtao Zhou. *AI-aided geometric design of anti-infection catheters*, Science Advances, January 2024, Vol. 10, Issue 1. https://doi.org/10.1126/sciadv.adj1741

Bentele, Riccardo and Rolf Weder. *On the Importance of Swiss Patient Data for Pharmaceutical R&D in Switzerland*, University of Basel - WWZ, April 2024.

Gen Z Broke the Marketing Funnel, Vogue Business, Archrival, 2024.

Roberts, Kevin. *Lovemarks*, powerHouse Books, 2005.

The 10 largest GDPR fines on Big Tech, TechCrunch, August 2024.

The discipline of innovation: making sure your innovation center actually makes your organization more innovative, CapGemini, 2017.

The future of gaming: An interview with Yat Siu, Chairman of the Board, Animoca Brands, The Cryptonomist, February 2024.

Chapter Three
AI and Generative AI: Shaping the Future of Total Marketing

Mara Cassinari

Total Marketing marks a significant shift from traditional marketing frameworks. As explained in Chapter 2, it extends the logic of Total Experience into a broader ecosystem where value is not just delivered but co-created. Whether it's customers, employees, digital interfaces, devices, or channels, every element plays a role in creating a seamless and interconnected experience. This means that marketing today must engage not only consumers, but also internal teams, partners, and digital systems, which we might call a stakeholder marketing approach. But how do you create personalized value across such a diverse range of touchpoints? And more importantly, how do you do it efficiently?

This is where technology takes the lead. Digital transformation is the foundation of Total Marketing, and it's powered by exponential technologies like AI, blockchain, and the intelligent use of data. These technologies allow us to go beyond products, building relationships that adapt and evolve in real time, thanks to continuous feedback from every corner of a business.

In this chapter, we'll discover the transformative role of Artificial Intelligence, particularly Generative AI, in shaping the future of marketing. How can brands go beyond merely selling and start co-creating with their audiences? How will devices and digital channels become the new face of customer engagement, replacing static touchpoints with intelligent, responsive systems?

So, as we explore AI's potential, do ask yourself: How can your organization embrace this new age of marketing where every stakeholder is connected, empowered, and engaged through technology? How do we ensure that this ecosystem remains healthy, inclusive, and generates value for all?

3.1. Introduction: A Brief Overview of AI and Generative AI

Artificial Intelligence has moved beyond just understanding and responding to human inputs; it now enables brands to create entirely new forms of interaction. With AI, marketing evolves from data analysis to co-creating experiences that are more personal, dynamic, and innovative.

Traditional AI, in simple terms, refers to technologies that can mimic human intelligence. These tools help us solve problems, make decisions, understand language, and identify patterns. For example, Netflix analyzes your viewing history and recommends shows, predicting content you might enjoy.[1]

Generative AI takes it a step further by not just recognizing patterns but creating entirely new content. Think about an AI that not only recognizes a picture of a cat, but can also generate entirely new images of cats that have never existed before. This opens endless possibilities for creative and innovative output, from text and video to music and art.

But how does it play in real life? Have you ever wondered how spam filters know which emails to block? Or how self-driving cars can spot pedestrians and stop signs? So, that's how AI acts; meanwhile, Gen AI, for example, powers deep fake videos, composes music, and helps create hyper-realistic digital art.

So, when do you turn to traditional AI and when is Gen AI the best option? Traditional AI is perfect for analyzing data, like sorting through customer feedback to identify common complaints or predicting equipment maintenance needs. Gen AI is ideal when you need to create something new, whether it's generating marketing slogans or helping overcome writer's block.

AI and Gen AI work together, complementing each other. While Artificial Intelligence helps us understand the world as it is, Generative AI helps us understand new possibilities.

Now, to make this even clearer, the table in the following page highlights the key differences, functionalities and industry applications for both AI and Gen AI. By seeing how it works, we can better understand how to leverage them for different tasks.

Total Marketing demands a seamless, interconnected approach, where every touchpoint, from customers to employees, evolves in real time. AI – especially Gen AI – allows brands to co-create dynamic, personalized value across this ecosystem. With these tools, brands don't just react to customer needs, but they anticipate and co-create experiences that evolve in real-time. Now, the challenge is: How can your brand move beyond selling to actively co-create with your audience, building truly personalized and engaging experiences?

---

[1] For more details on how Netflix's recommendation system works, you can visit their research page https://research.netflix.com/research-area/recommendations.

Table 3.1: Comparative Overview of AI and Gen AI.

	Artificial Intelligence	**Generative AI**
Description	AI includes a wide range of technologies that let machines simulate human intelligence. This involves tasks like problem-solving, decision-making, language understanding, and pattern recognition.	A specialized type of AI that focuses on creating new content or patterns based on the data it has learned. Instead of just recognizing patterns, Gen AI produces new outputs like images, text, or audio.
Functionality	Uses data patterns to classify, predict and make decisions, producing results that people can use.	Uses data to generate new outputs like images, audio, and text that people can understand.
Use Cases	Fraud detection, customer service chatbots, predictive maintenance, autonomous vehicles, and language translation.	Image and video generation, text generation (e.g., Chat GPT), music composition, customer journey mapping, and content creation (e.g., articles, marketing copy).
Example	AI in fraud detection systems analyzes transaction patterns to flag potential fraud. AI chatbots provide customer service by understanding and responding to user queries.	Generative AI models like DALL-E, by OpenAI, create new images based on textual descriptions. Generative AI in analyzing and synthesizing large volumes of customer data to create detailed, personalized journey maps.
Data Processing Example	AI processes sensor data from machines to predict when they might fail.	Generative AI turns raw data (e.g., pixel brightness in images) into human-readable formats (e.g., images).
Pattern Recognition Example	AI in healthcare systems can spot patterns in medical records that suggest a high risk for diseases.	Generative AI can create new art pieces by learning from a dataset of existing artworks.
Industry Applications	Finance: fraud detection, algorithmic trading. Healthcare: diagnostic systems, patient monitoring. Retail: inventory management, recommendation systems. Automotive: self-driving cars, predictive maintenance.	Art and design: creating new artworks, fashion designs. Media and entertainment: generating movie scripts, deepfake technology. Education: creating personalized learning materials. Scientific research: simulating chemical reactions, generating synthetic data for experiments.

3.2. Personalized Interactions: Enhancing Customer Experience with AI

As customer behaviors and expectations are constantly evolving, people expect business to know their preferences before they even express them. Personalization has become the foundation of successful business strategies, but it's about more than just addressing a customer by name. It means truly understanding their needs, anticipating what they'll want, and delivering tailored experiences to create a lasting impact.

Traditional AI plays a key role in making this transformation possible. Through machine learning and predictive analytics, companies can craft interactions that resonate with individual customers, offering experiences that feel unique and relevant at every touchpoint. This approach builds customer loyalty, ensuring that customers feel valued and understood in every interaction.

It doesn't stop here. Generative AI pushes this personalization further by creating dynamic, real-time content tailored specifically to individual customers. Whether it's customizing marketing messages or generating new content in response to customer interaction, Gen AI delivers fresh, engaging experiences that strengthen the connection between business and their audiences.

3.2.1. Traditional AI Techniques

AI transforms how businesses engage with their customers by analyzing data and recognizing patterns, enabling more personal and effective interactions.

Data analysis and predictive insights

Think of AI as a detective, uncovering customer preferences and trends through data analytics. This allows businesses to offer tailored experiences that resonate with individual customers. For instance, an online retailer where you frequently purchase moisturizers and serums might suggest complementary products, such as a new face mask or sunscreen that align with your skincare routine. Beyond this, predictive analytics can go further by analyzing seasonal trends and your buying patterns to anticipate when you'll need to restock. As a result, the retailer may proactively offer a discount on your favorite moisturizer just as you're running low, or recommend a newly launched product that fits your preferences, enhancing the overall shopping experience.

Customer segmentation

AI excels at grouping customers into distinctive segments based on their behaviors, preferences and demographic data, enabling businesses to deliver more targeted communications. A fitness brand might analyze some purchase and engagement data to identify two key segments: casual gym-goers and dedicated athletes.

The casual gym-goers may receive promotions for comfortable, stylish activewear and beginner fitness programs, while the dedicated athletes could be offered high-performance supplements and advanced training routines. This tailored approach ensures that each customer receives messaging that is aligned with their fitness goals, increasing their engagement.

Real-time personalization

With AI, personalization can happen on the fly. A streaming service could suggest movies based on what you've just watched, making each recommendation feel timely and relevant and keeping you engaged for longer.

Sentiment analysis

By interpreting the emotional tone behind interactions, such as emails or social media posts, AI allows businesses to respond in a more empathetic and personalized way. For example, a beauty brand could analyze your feedback to offer solutions that address both preferences and concerns, improving overall satisfaction.

3.2.2. Generative AI for Dynamic Content Customization

Generative AI is changing how businesses create and manage content by producing new personalized content in real-time. While traditional AI excels at analyzing data and making predictions, Generative AI goes further by creating content that is tailored to different audiences' needs and preferences. This brings personalization to a new level.

Imagine visiting a website where every product you see feels like it was made just for you. Generative AI makes this possible by constantly adapting to your behavior and interests and ensuring a more engaging and relevant experience.

Website personalization

Gen AI doesn't just recommend products based on past behavior; it reshapes your browsing experience as you go. If you're always searching for eco-friendly products, the website could highlight not only green products but also generate articles and user stories about sustainability. It's like having a personal shopper who understands your values and defines content accordingly.

Real-time marketing adjustments

Live marketing campaigns benefit significantly from real-time adjustments made possible by Gen AI. Imagine a fashion retailer dynamically changing ads based on current weather in your location, showcasing cozy sweaters and raincoats when it's cold and rainy, while, on a sunny day, they might promote summer dresses and sunglasses. This keeps marketing content fresh and relevant, making it more likely to capture attention, driving higher engagement and conversion rates.

Interactive multimodal experiences powered by Gen AI

Generative AI is transforming how users interact with content by enabling multimodal experiences. Imagine reading an article on your phone, and with just a tap on an image, instantly receiving additional information like location details or related facts, without leaving the article. You could ask follow-up questions to dive deeper into a topic, getting real-time answers while seamlessly returning to your reading. This capability allows for highly personalized, interactive experiences, making the information retrieval intuitive and tailored to each user's needs.

Interactive user interfaces

In today's digital landscape, interactivity is key. Generative AI doesn't just recommend actions, it generates dynamic, personalized interfaces that respond to your inputs in real-time. Think of a fitness app that generates personalized workout plans tailored to your fitness level, progress and goals. If you had a high-intensity workout yesterday, it might suggest a light routine today, keeping you motivated and healthy.

Content creation and management

Generative AI shines in automating content creation. Imagine receiving marketing emails or social media posts that feel as if they were written just for you.

In customer support, Gen AI can create personalized troubleshooting guides based on your product history, making it easier and quicker for you to self-solve your issues.

In education, AI adapts learning materials to your pace and style, helping you overcome difficulties with personalized exercises and quizzes, ensuring that you grasp complex subjects more effectively.

In the healthcare industry, Generative AI can be used to create personalized wellness plans based on a patient's medical history, lifestyle, and preferences. For example, AI could generate tailored exercise routines, dietary suggestions, and medication reminders, ensuring that the plan adapts to real-time changes in the patient's condition or daily activity. This level of personalization helps healthcare providers offer more targeted care, improving patients' health, while saving time on manual adjustments to care plans.

Together, AI and Generative AI are transforming how businesses engage with their audiences by delivering deeper personalization and dynamic content. As these technologies evolve, they enable companies to move beyond standard techniques, creating more meaningful and real-time connections with customers. This shift is key in the broader vision of Total Marketing, where the focus is on delivering value at every interaction, in an interconnected ecosystem.

Table 3.2: The role of AI in personalization: Comparing traditional and generative approaches.

Aspect	Traditional AI	Generative AI
Content Personalization	Analyzes past customer data to recommend products and content.	Creates fresh, personalized content in real-time based on current user behavior.
Real-Time Customization	Offers static suggestions based on historical data.	Updates content in response to immediate user interests and actions.
Interactivity	Provides suggestions based on past behaviors.	Generates personalized, interactive experiences in real-time.
Marketing Adjustments	Suggests changes to campaigns; usually requires manual adjustments.	Automatically generates and adapts marketing content in real-time.
Customer Support	Provides automated responses based on past interaction data.	Provides personalized troubleshooting guides based on unique users' interactions.
Educational Content	Recommends resources based on progress and performance.	Creates custom study plans and exercises tailored to individual learning needs.
Benefits	Enhances engagement with relevant suggestions.	Deepens personalization with dynamic content-aware context.
	Improves customer satisfaction through timely, data-driven suggestions.	Increases engagement and loyalty by offering dynamic, personalized experiences.

3.3. Optimizing Employee Experience Through Automation

The integration of AI technologies into the workplace has transformed how businesses operate, particularly in automating employees' tasks. Traditional AI and Robotic Process Automation (RPA) streamline repetitive processes, greatly improving efficiency and accuracy. Generative AI goes a step further by supporting creative and complex activities, adding a layer of innovation to task automation. Together, these technologies reduce the manual workload for employees, allowing them to focus on more strategic and creative endeavors. This dual approach helps organizations foster a more productive and engaged workforce while delivering superior service and personalized experiences to clients.

3.3.1. Traditional AI for Task Automation and RPA

RPA is changing how businesses handle routine tasks by using software systems that emulate human interactions with digital systems. These "digital FTEs" perform tasks like data entry, scheduling or data processing without human intervention. By automating these routine tasks, RPA frees employees to focus on strategic, creative activities, boosting productivity and job satisfaction.

RPA enhances service support by processing orders instantly, reducing wait times, while in finance, it speeds up tasks like loan processing, improving customer satisfaction. Robotic Process Automation operates with significantly higher speed and accuracy than human workers, reducing errors, and scaling operations during peak times without the need for additional staff.[2]

In the tech industry, AI-powered scheduling and project management tools automate administrative tasks such as meeting scheduling and task allocation. For instance, an AI tool can automatically schedule meetings based on participants' availability, send reminders, and update project timelines in real-time. This automation reduces administrative overhead and ensures that projects stay on track. Leading companies like IBM have implemented RPA to streamline project management tasks, saving time and improving efficiency.

AI in HR: Recruitment, onboarding, and employee engagement

AI is reshaping HR processes, making it easier for organizations to attract, engage, and retain people.

- Talent attraction: AI chatbots engage potential candidates from the start, answering questions and guiding them through the pre-application process. This improves talent engagement and increases the likelihood of successful applications. For instance, IBM's Watson Candidate Assistant tripled conversion rates by providing tailored information and immediate responses to candidate queries.[3]

- Hiring process: AI speeds up recruitment by automating resume screening, predicting job performance, and identifying the best candidates. It also helps reduce bias by focusing on skills and qualifications. As a result, companies can reduce time-to-hire and increase the quality of candidates.

- Employee engagement: AI provides managers with actionable insights into team dynamics and individual needs. AI tools analyze feedback, monitor social interactions within the company, and notify managers

---

[2] Gartner, *Peer Connect Perspectives: Robotic Process Automation Use Cases. 2019.* https://www.gartner.com/en/documents/3978927. This Gartner content is archived and is included for historical context only.

[3] Nigel Guenole and Sheir Feinzig, *The business case of AI in HR,* IBM, October 2021. IBM compared its Watson Candidate Assistant (WCA) with a traditional static website, the conversion rate from exploration to application was 36% for WCA, compared to 12% for the traditional website.

about important developments. This proactive management approach helps address issues before they escalate, improving overall engagement and satisfaction. Higher employee satisfaction scores and reduced turnover rates are common outcomes when AI is effectively utilized for employee engagement.

- Employee retention: AI supports smarter compensation planning and career development opportunities. By analyzing market trends and individual performance, AI recommends competitive and fair compensation packages tailored for each employee, improving retention rates and enhancing satisfaction with compensation and career development.

- Personalized learning: AI facilitates personalized learning by recommending courses and training programs tailored to individual needs and career goals. Platforms like IBM's Your Learning provide personalized learning paths, making learning more relevant and accessible. Higher course completion rates and improved skill gap closure are typical benefits of AI-driven personalized learning.

- People development: AI-powered career coaching tools guide employees through career transitions and growth opportunities, offering personalized career advice. This supports long-term career satisfaction and increases internal mobility, helping employees stay motivated and competitive in their roles.

By leveraging AI throughout the HR lifecycle, from recruitment to employee development, organizations can create more efficient, personalized, and engaging employee experiences. This boosts productivity and helps retain top talent, resulting in a more motivated and satisfied workforce.

3.3.2. Generative AI for Creative Task Automation

Gen AI does more than just automate routine tasks; it empowers businesses to perform creative and complex activities. By generating content, designing marketing materials, and enhancing customer journey mapping, Generative AI supports employees in areas that demand creativity and innovation.

AI tools generating content for journalism

Gen AI is reshaping journalism by providing powerful tools that assist rather than replace journalists. While some worry that AI might take over human jobs, the preference for human-written news, particularly for serious topics, remains strong. AI, however, enhances journalistic workflows in several impactful ways:[4]

---

[4] Monica Attard et al., *Gen AI and Journalism*, UTS, April 9, 2024.

- Summarizing documents: AI helps by quickly summarizing lengthy reports and documents, enabling journalists to grasp essential information faster.

- Story structuring: AI can also suggest the best way to structure stories, making the writing process more efficient.

- Generating reader-focused questions: AI can even generate lists of questions that readers might want answered, ensuring the content is engaging and thorough.

- Visual content creation and automated reporting: Journalists can now describe the visualizations they need, and AI will generate charts, infographics, and other visual aids. This makes data-driven storytelling more accessible, especially for those without advanced data skills.

- Editing and personalization: AI can critically review articles, suggest improvements, and identify any inconsistencies. This ensures that the final content is polished and comprehensive. Additionally, journalists can write a broad overview and then use AI to tailor the content for specific audiences, adding technical details for experts or simplifying language for children.

While AI excels at reorganizing and presenting existing information, true journalism requires creativity, original thought, and investigative qualities, which are skills that AI supports but does not replace, at least for now.

The BBC's AI innovation

As of February 2024, the BBC has launched 12 pilot projects to explore how Generative AI can enhance content creation and improve operational efficiency.[5]

To maximize content value, news articles are being translated into multiple languages, led by BBC News, to make content accessible to a broader audience. Additionally, live sports radio commentaries are being transformed into text for BBC Sports live pages, ensuring timely updates and wider accessibility.

For creating new audience experiences, journalists are being equipped with AI tools like a 'headline helper' that suggests headlines and article summaries, streamlining the writing process. AI is also being implemented for better content labeling and retrieval, helping teams quickly find and repurpose content for new projects.

The BBC emphasizes using AI responsibly, updating its Editorial Guidance to ensure AI usage aligns with its editorial values and maintains audience trust.

---

[5] Rhodri Talfan Davies, *An update on the BBC's plans for Generative AI (Gen AI) and how we plan to use AI tools responsibly*, BBC, February 28, 2024. Accessible at: https://www.bbc.com/mediacentre/articles/2024/update-generative-ai-and-ai-tools-bbc.

Human oversight is a key part of this strategy to prevent misuse and ensure accuracy.

Gen AI is transforming customer journeys

Customer journey mapping is an essential practice for understanding and improving the Customer Experience. By visualizing how customers interact with a brand, businesses can identify pain points and opportunities for improvement. AI technologies, particularly Generative AI, are revolutionizing this process, making it faster, more personalized and insightful.

AI enhances customer journey mapping by capturing and analyzing vast amounts of data, providing a more detailed and accurate representation of the Customer Experience. It can identify patterns and trends that humans might overlook, offering insights into customer behaviors and preferences that help companies create more tailored engagement strategies at every touchpoint.

AI-driven customer journey in Banking

Imagine a prospective customer wanting to open a bank account. AI optimizes every stage of this journey to provide a smoother, more efficient experience.

- Awareness: Generative AI analyzes online behavior to understand how potential customers can discover the bank. Using sentiment analysis and data mining, AI identifies the most effective marketing channels, tailoring ads based on browsing history and behavior to increase engagement and click-through rates.

- Consideration: AI chatbots and virtual assistants respond to customers' queries in real-time, offering personalized product comparisons and scheduling follow-up interactions. This ensures the customer feels supported throughout their decision-making process, enhancing customer support.

- Decision: AI automates document verification and fraud detection, using machine learning algorithms to quickly authenticate documents and pre-filled forms, enhancing completion rates and reducing errors.

- Service: Once the account is open, AI-driven virtual assistants provide personalized financial advice based on the customer's spending and saving patterns. This improves setup completion rates and customer satisfaction scores.

- Engagement and retention: After the account is established, AI continues to monitor customer interactions, identifying opportunities for proactive engagement. It suggests features or products based on a customer's behavior, boosting satisfaction and retention rates.

Table 3.3: Human vs AI-driven process in banking.

Phase	Human Process	AI-Driven Process	Timing	Benefits
Awareness and Initial Research	Customers see the bank's ad and visit the website to learn more.	AI delivers personalized ads based on browsing behavior and sentiment analysis.	Human: Weeks for campaign design. AI: Instantaneous personalization.	Improved click-through rate, enhanced brand awareness, and targeted advertising.
Consideration: Exploration and Comparison	The customer visits the bank's website and contacts customer service for more details.	AI provides personalized content, and virtual assistants answer complex questions in real-time.	Human: Minutes to hours for customer service response. AI: Immediate personalized response.	Faster information retrieval, higher satisfaction, and reduced need for manual service.
Decision-Making	The customer decides to open an account and starts the application process.	AI pre-fills forms, automates document verification, and expedites the application process.	Human: Days to weeks for form completion. AI: A Few minutes to complete the application.	Higher conversion rates, reduced errors, and faster processing time.
Service: Account Setup and Personalization	The customer personalizes their account with human assistance.	AI guides the setup, offering tailored tips based on customer data.	Human: Minutes to hours for setup completion. AI: Quick and efficient setup.	Increased satisfaction through personalization, reduced setup errors.
Engagement and Retention	Customer interacts with the bank, uses services, and contacts support when needed.	AI proactively monitors activity and offers personalized recommendations, reducing customer churn.	Human: Varies (hours to days for issue resolution). AI: Real-time monitoring and support-	Increased customer loyalty, higher retention, and proactive engagement reducing churn.

The comparison (in the table in the previous page) highlights the significant advantages AI offers over traditional human-driven processes, particularly in terms of speed, personalization and efficiency. Thanks to the automation of key stages of the customer journey, banks can reduce operational costs and enhance the Customer Experience, driving higher engagement, satisfaction, and retention.

3.4. Enabling Product Usability, Innovation, and User Experience

The intersection of Artificial Intelligence and product design is reshaping how businesses create and refine their offerings. AI has evolved from a tool for automation into a catalyst for innovation, enhancing usability, functionality, and the overall experience. By leveraging both traditional AI and Generative AI, companies can significantly improve their product development processes, from initial design concepts to market-ready solutions.

3.4.1. Traditional AI for Optimizing Product Design and Functionality

Artificial Intelligence is transforming how we approach product usability and UX. Through AI, companies can optimize product designs and improve functionality and user behavior by crafting more intuitive, user-friendly, and efficient products that meet the evolving needs of users.

AI technologies are incredible tools for analyzing vast amounts of user interaction data. They help identify patterns and behaviors that inform better design decisions. For instance, AI-powered tools like Google Analytics track user behavior such as clicks, time spent on sections, and bounce rates, providing real-time insights to refine product design and improve user experience.

Beyond design, AI significantly optimized product functionality. A McKinsey report shows that companies using AI for design optimization have seen a 20% increase in user satisfaction and a 15% reduction in design iteration time.[6] This makes interfaces more intuitive, reducing the learning curve for new users and increasing user engagement and conversions.

AI doesn't just stop at design; it also optimizes product functionality. Features like voice and image recognition allow users to interact with products naturally and hands-free. Devices like Amazon's Alexa and Apple's Siri demonstrate how AI-driven voice assistants can simplify everyday tasks for a broader audience, including individuals with disabilities.

---

[6] Bryce Booth et al., *Generative AI fuels creative physical product design but is no magic wand*, McKinsey, 2024.

Additionally, AI can optimize product performance through predictive maintenance, analyzing data from sensors in machinery to forecast potential failures and schedule maintenance before breakdowns occur. Siemens applies AI in predictive maintenance by blending machine sensor data with human input to anticipate equipment issues before they arise.[7] The AI analyzes historical data to detect patterns, enabling maintenance teams to take proactive steps. By incorporating insights from maintenance records and user feedback, the system delivers a more comprehensive view of machine performance. This helps minimize downtime, extend the lifespan of the equipment, and make maintenance processes more efficient and accessible for both new and expert users.

Smart home devices are a perfect example of how AI enhances usability. Take Google Nest, for instance, a smart thermostat that uses AI to learn user preferences and automatically adjust the home's temperature.[8] By integrating voice and image recognition technologies, Google Nest personalizes the environment, ensuring optimal comfort and energy efficiency. Over time, it fine-tunes settings based on habits and patterns, creating a seamless and convenient experience tailored to each household. This blend of automation and personalization demonstrates how AI transforms everyday living into a smarter, more responsive environment.

3.4.2. Generative AI for Prototyping and Testing New Product Ideas

Gen AI is a game-changer in driving innovation across various business sectors. It transforms content creation, accelerates product development, creates innovative applications, and revolutionizes marketing strategies.

In product design, this technology redefines the entire process, making it more creative and efficient. Starting with market research, AI quickly finds hidden opportunities and understands what consumers really want, enabling teams to gather and analyze data much faster than before.

In the concept development stage, Generative AI can create new, realistic images that inspire designers to explore bold and unique ideas. This reduces the time spent on tedious tasks like making concept images and mood boards, allowing teams to focus more on creativity.

Additionally, this technology significantly speeds up the product development cycle by enabling rapid prototyping and testing. Traditionally, product

---

[7] The information in this section is based on details available on the Siemens website, specifically from the Predictive Maintenance section. For more information visit https://www.siemens.com.

[8] For more information see Google's website https://store.google.com/.

development often involves time-consuming and costly iterations. With AI-driven design tools, companies can simulate and test new ideas. For instance, AI can take initial product concepts and produce 3D models, allowing designers to evaluate and refine ideas. Before physical prototypes are created, AI simulations predict product performance under different conditions, identifying potential issues early in the development process and saving both time and resources.

McKinsey estimates that Generative AI can reduce product development cycle times by up to 70%, and they report a striking example that comes from the automotive industry, where industrial designers at a leading OEM [9] employed Generative AI to create 25 variations of next-generation car dashboard designs in just two hours.[10] Without AI, producing such detailed and high-quality variations would have taken at least a week, highlighting the significant time and effort savings enabled by this technology. This efficiency allows teams to focus on refining and testing the most promising designs, aligning them with the company's vision and manufacturability standards.

When refining concepts, AI helps designers polish product styles and plan future ideas in hours rather than weeks. Finally, during concept testing, AI brings ideas to life, making it easier for business leaders and consumers to discuss and provide feedback. This helps ensure that new products meet market needs and have a better chance of success.

AI's ability to analyze user behavior in real-time provides actionable insights for improving user experience. Adobe Sensei GenAI enables brands to leverage advanced machine learning to process data from customer interactions, identifying areas where users face difficulties and suggesting tailored changes to make the interface more user-friendly.[11] By analyzing user behavior across digital touchpoints, this tool helps businesses refine their digital experiences to meet specific customer needs. For instance, if a user frequently abandons a shopping cart, Sensei GenAI can generate personalized content or product recommendations to re-engage the customer, ensuring that UX evolves based on real-time data and customer preferences.

Generative AI is a key driver for innovation, accelerating product development, refining user experiences, and helping companies stay competitive in a fast-changing market.

---

[9] Original Equipment Manufacturer.

[10] Bryce Booth et al., *Generative AI fuels creative physical product design but is no magic wand*, McKinsey, 2024.

[11] For more details on Adobe Sensei GenAI and its capabilities, visit Adobe's website https://business.adobe.com/.

3.5. Enhancing User Interactions Across Multiple Platforms

Multiexperience plays a vital role in how brands engage with customers across various platforms. AI and Gen AI can significantly enhance these interactions by integrating text, voice, and visual inputs into a unified customer journey. In Total Marketing, AI ensures multifaceted, consistent, personalized engagement across multiple touchpoints, particularly in customer service. From chatbots and virtual assistants to augmented reality (AR) applications, AI-driven solutions handle complex queries and drive more effective marketing campaigns and customer engagement.

3.5.1. Seamless AI-Driven Multimodal Interactions

AI-driven multimodal interactions are transforming brand communication. AI-powered chatbots, for example, can engage customers through text on a website, voice on a smart speaker, or visual elements on a mobile app. This unified experience strengthens Total Marketing efforts by maintaining consistent messaging and branding across all channels. Moreover, AI provides contextual responses based on past behaviors, which allows for more personalized service that resonates with the target audience, increasing customer satisfaction and loyalty.

Optimizing user engagement across platforms

AI's integration into Multiexperience strategies helps brands maintain consistent communication across channels. This enables brands to optimize user engagement and leverage insights from AI-driven data analytics to fine-tune marketing efforts and maximize impact. By reducing friction points in the user journey, AI improves overall customer satisfaction and contributes to more effective marketing outcomes.

AI in augmented reality: The IKEA App Example

The IKEA Place app exemplifies how AI and augmented reality elevate the shopping experience.[12] Customers can place virtual furniture in their homes, previewing how different pieces fit in their space. The app's AI analyzes room dimensions and provides personalized recommendations, making the shopping process highly interactive and engaging. This app bridges the gap between online and physical shopping, offering a convenient and immersive experience tailored to individual needs.

Connecting the dots: AI's Role in Multiexperience

AI technologies, like the IKEA Place app, demonstrate how advanced interaction can transform customer engagement. By embracing AI and multimodal

---

[12] For further details about the IKEA App, visit IKEA's website: https://www.ikea.com/.

interactions, businesses can create deeper connections with their audience, offering a personalized and enjoyable journey. This approach not only meets the evolving customer demands but also sets a new standard for managing digital interactions.

3.5.2. Crafting the Ideal Multiexperience Journey: Generative AI and a Multi-Modal Chatbot in Action

Generative AI and multi-modal chatbots take Total Marketing to the next level by enabling hyper-personalized, real-time, and context-aware interactions across platforms. These technologies create seamless journeys that drive more effective marketing strategies and customer experiences.

Step-by-step ideal journey:

1. **Scanning the living room with AR (Augmented Reality).** Picture this: you're at home, ready to redecorate your living room. You open an augmented reality app on your smartphone, which uses advanced AR features to scan your living room. Generative AI analyzes the room layout and recommends furniture that aligns with your taste, blending seamlessly with the existing décor. This personalized marketing approach helps build stronger customer relationships.

2. **Designing the new space with AI assistance.** Next, log in to your personalized design portal on your laptop. Here, you see the AI-generated design suggestions. As you begin designing your new space using the 3D model, a multi-modal chatbot appears on the screen. This chatbot can interact through text, voice, and even visual cues. You can speak to it, type questions, or use hand gestures to indicate areas you want to change. The chatbot understands and assists in real-time, offering alternatives, providing style tips, and ensuring your design aligns with your preferences.

3. **Making purchases online and in-store.** With your design finalized, you decide to purchase some items online for home delivery and visit the store for others. AI helps you compile your shopping list, suggests the best time for store visits based on crowd predictions, and even reserves items to ensure they are in stock. As you shop online, the chatbot guides you, confirming compatibility with your design and offering additional recommendations based on your choices.

4. **Collecting products in-store with AR navigation.** At the store, AR navigation guides you to each item on your list, while the multi-modal chatbot is available to answer any questions you might have. For example, you can ask about the sustainability of a product, and the chatbot will provide detailed information. It can also connect with an

employee if you need more in-depth assistance. The chatbot ensures your shopping experience is efficient and informative, enhancing your interaction with both the technology and the store staff.

5. **Installing furniture with AI-driven support.** Back home, it's time to install your new furniture. The app provides detailed, interactive assembly instructions. If you encounter any issues, the multi-modal chatbot is there to help. You can show the problem using your smartphone camera, and it provides real-time visual and verbal guidance. If needed, it escalates the query to a human expert, ensuring prompt and effective support.

Connecting the ideal Multiexperience journey to Total Marketing

Throughout this journey, AI plays a key role in delivering personalized, seamless interactions at every stage. By analyzing real-time data, AI tailors each touchpoint to customer preferences, ensuring consistency and convenience. This approach aligns Total Marketing with operational efficiency, enhancing customer interaction and driving operational success.

3.6. Case Studies: AI in Total Marketing

The rise of Artificial Intelligence and Generative AI has reshaped industries, transforming customer experiences and revolutionizing how businesses engage with their audiences.

Leading companies like Walmart, Bank of America, and Toyota are integrating these technologies into their marketing strategies, showcasing the transformative potential of AI across different sectors. They demonstrate their potential to drive personalization, efficiency, and satisfaction within a Total Marketing approach.

As in Chapter 1, the following examples show how different companies use AI in ways that reflect specific goals and contexts; there's no one-size-fits-all formula, but plenty of inspiration.

3.6.1. Walmart's Comprehensive AI and Generative AI Integration

Walmart is at the forefront of leveraging AI and Gen AI to reshape the retail landscape, driving efficiency and personalization across its platforms. This approach enhances operational efficiency while delivering a more personalized shopping experience, thanks to AI-driven inventory management and adaptive retail strategies.

AI in inventory management

Walmart is transforming inventory management by harnessing the power of AI, Generative AI, and robotics, ensuring customers always find the products they need.

Walmart's AI-powered inventory management system leverages historical data and predictive analytics to strategically place items across distribution centers and stores, anticipating demand and improving product availability. The system continuously learns and adapts, correcting supply chain inefficiencies and aligning inventory flow with regional preferences.[13]

Sam's Club, a division of Walmart, takes this a step further with the deployment of Inventory Scan technology in partnership with Brain Corp and Tennant Company. This solution integrates inventory scanning capabilities into nearly 600 autonomous floor scrubbers. These AI-powered robots autonomously navigate stores and gather and analyze pricing accuracy, stock levels, and product placement. This efficiency reduces waste and inventory loss, allowing associates to focus more on providing excellent customer service.[14]

AI in adaptive retail

Walmart is also leading the way in creating adaptive retail experiences, using AI and Generative AI to create personalized shopping experiences.

- Virtual try-on technology: Walmart's Zeekit virtual try-on platform allows customers to visualize how clothing will look on them using their own photos, creating more interactive customer interactions. The platform's new Be Your Own Model feature enhances this experience by offering ultra-realistic simulations, showing how clothing drapes and fits on a customer's unique body shape[15].

- Scan & Go app: Sam's Club members can skip the checkout line using the Scan & Go app, where items are scanned during shopping, paid for within the app, and verified at exit using AI-powered vision technology. The app includes seamless exit technology, which uses AI and computer vision to identify and verify the items in members' carts,

---

[13] Parvez Musani, *Decking the aisles with data: How Walmart's AI-powered inventory system brightens the holidays*, Walmart Global Tech, October 25, 2023. Available at: https://tech.walmart.com/content/walmart-global-tech/en_us/blog/post/walmarts-ai-powered-inventory-system-brightens-the-holidays.html.

[14] *Sam's Club Begins National Deployment of Automated Inventory Analytics Robots*, Walmart, January, 27, 2022. Available at: https://corporate.walmart.com/about/samsclub/news/2022/01/27/sams-club-begins-national-deployment-of-automated-inventory-analytics-robots.

[15] Denise Incandela, *Walmart Levels Up Virtual Try-On for Apparel With Be Your Own Model Experience*, Walmart, 2022. Available at: https://corporate.walmart.com/news/2022/09/15/walmart-levels-up-virtual-try-on-for-apparel-with-be-your-own-model-experience.

further streamlining the shopping journey and eliminating the need for manual receipt verification.[16]

- Generative AI-powered search: Customers can now ask natural language queries like "Help me plan a football watch party" and receive curated product recommendations.[17] This personalized search capability makes the buying process simpler and more intuitive, enhancing decision-making and engagement.

Walmart's strategic integration of AI and Gen AI not only improves operational efficiency but also enhances the overall experience by providing data-driven, personalized recommendations across touchpoints. Whether through inventory management or adaptive retail strategies, AI enhances customer engagement by delivering what customers want, when and where they need it.

- AI-driven inventory systems ensure product availability and accuracy, while personalized features like virtual try-ons and Gen AI-powered search make shopping more engaging and tailored to individual preferences.

- Automation of routine inventory tasks frees associates to focus on high-value customer interactions, improving both service quality and employee satisfaction.

- Gen AI-powered tools streamline the shopping process, making it easier for users to navigate and interact with Walmart's digital platforms.

- Walmart's integration of online and offline retail strategies, such as virtual try-ons and the Scan & Go app, creates a cohesive experience that bridges digital and physical shopping environments.

Walmart's application of AI in both inventory management and customer-facing technologies demonstrates the transformative impact of AI in retail. These innovations help Walmart strengthen its marketing strategies by combining operational efficiency with personalized, data-driven customer engagement.

---

[16] *AI-powered convenience: The evolution of Scan & Go,* Walmart, 2024. Available at: https://tech.walmart.com/content/walmart-global-tech/en_us/blog/post/skip-the-check out-line-with-scan-and-go-at-sams-club.html.

[17] *Walmart's Generative AI search puts more time back in customers' hands,* Walmart 2024. Available at: https://tech.walmart.com/content/walmart-global-tech/en_us/blog/post/ walmarts-generative-ai-search-puts-more-time-back-in-customers-hands.html.

3.6.2. Erica: Bank of America's AI-Powered Virtual Assistant

Artificial intelligence is transforming the banking and financial sector, bringing unprecedented changes in how banks operate and interact with customers. By harnessing the power of AI, banks can now provide personalized, efficient, and accessible services around the clock. One of the standout innovations in this space is Bank of America's (BoA) AI-powered virtual assistant, Erica.

Launched in June 2018, Erica has become a cornerstone of Bank of America's digital strategy, changing customer interaction with the bank. Erica is not just a chatbot; it's a comprehensive virtual financial assistant designed to help customers manage their finances more effectively. Erica serves as a financial advisor available 24/7, ready to assist with tasks ranging from checking balances to providing complex financial insights.[18]

How Erica works

Interacting with Erica is seamless and user-friendly. Customers with a Bank of America account and the BoA Mobile Banking app can log in and engage with Erica through text or voice commands. Erica's icon is clearly displayed on the app's home screen, allowing for effortless engagement. This intuitive design ensures a smooth, integrated experience by making each interaction part of a cohesive customer journey.

Erica leverages advanced analytics and AI-driven messaging technologies to provide personalized financial assistance. It can analyze a range of data within Bank of America, including cash flow, balances, transaction history, and upcoming bills. This comprehensive data consideration helps users stay on top of their finances, offering personalized insights and proactive financial management advice.

Unique capabilities of Erica

As of April 2024, Erica has facilitated over two billion interactions since its launch, with two million daily engagements. Erica is enriched with features that make managing finances straightforward and efficient.[19] For instance, it integrates with BoA's Spending & Budgeting tool, helping users review spending habits, compare income against expenditures, and set saving goals. Erica acts like a personal finance coach, offering timely advice and alerts.

---

[18] The data and information about Erica and Bank of America's AI initiatives were sourced from Bank of America's official newsroom. *BofA's Erica Surpasses 2 Billion Interactions, Helping 42 Million Clients Since Launch*, Bank of America, April 2024. Accessible at: https://newsroom.bankofamerica.com/content/newsroom/press-releases/2024/04/bofa-s-erica-surpasses-2-billion-interactions--helping-42-millio.html.

[19] Ibid.

Erica can also monitor and manage recurring subscriptions, provide insights into spending behavior, and keep users informed about deposits and refunds. For example, if someone has spent more than usual in a month, Erica can alert them if it predicts their account balance might run low, helping to avoid overdrafts.

One of Erica's standout features is its ability to connect customers directly with human customer service agents when necessary. This ensures that if a question arises that Erica can't answer, the customer is seamlessly transferred to a human agent, who can resolve the issue quickly and efficiently.

Additionally, Erica supports customers in managing their investment portfolios by helping access quotes, track performance, and place trades, while also connecting users with a Merrill advisor for more personalized investment guidance — all from the Mobile Banking app.

Beyond financial management, Erica keeps users informed about changes to their credit score through alerts and helps monitor Zelle payments. Zelle is a peer-to-peer (P2P) payment service that allows users to send and receive money quickly using just an email address or mobile phone number. Additionally, customers can lock and unlock their credit and debit cards via Erica, providing an added layer of security, especially if cards are misplaced or fraudulent activity is suspected.

Moreover, Erica assists users in viewing and redeeming rewards in one place, simplifying the process of managing various rewards and benefits associated with their accounts.

Overall benefits of Erica

Erica represents a significant step forward in customer engagement by delivering efficient, personalized and proactive services. Its ability to offer over 30 proactive insights monthly demonstrates the power of AI in anticipating customer needs, with millions of insights provided around subscription management, spending behavior, and account charges.[20]

Customers consistently benefit from Erica's fast and accurate responses, with 98 percent of users receiving the help they need within an average of 44 seconds. For more complex inquiries, BoA's Mobile Chat ensures customers are connected to live representatives, ensuring seamlessly AI-driven support with human expertise.[21]

For employees, Erica significantly reduces the workload by managing common inquiries, allowing them to focus on more complex and engaging

---

[20] Ibid.

[21] Ibid.

tasks that require a human touch. This shift not only boosts productivity but also enhances job satisfaction, leading to a better overall experience for both customers and employees. Tools like Banker Assist, which aggregate client insights, further enable employees to provide superior service.

Erica ensures a consistent experience across various platforms and devices, whether through mobile apps, chats, or other digital channels. This uniformity aligns with Total Marketing principles, ensuring that every interaction contributes to a cohesive, customer-centric experience.

By continuously improving with over 50,000 updates since its launch, Erica remains a leader in AI innovation, driving both customer satisfaction and operational efficiency with Bank of America.[22]

3.6.3. Toyota and Generative AI: Enhancing the Future of Mobility

Artificial intelligence has significantly reshaped various industries, and the automotive sector is no exception. At Toyota, AI is more than a futuristic vision but a core element in advancing safety, quality and Customer Experience. By integrating both AI and generative AI into its operations, Toyota is playing a leading role in innovations that meet evolving technological advancements and customer expectations.

Toyota's initial goal in 2016 was to engineer a resilient cloud safety system, which led to the development of Safety Connect, powered by Drivelink from Toyota Connected North America (TCNA).[23] Safety Connect uses telematics data to detect collisions and automatically notify call center agents, ensuring quick response times even if the driver is unconscious.

Parallelly, TCNA engineers explored AI-driven services, resulting in the 2021 launch of virtual agents like "Hey Toyota" and "Hey Lexus." These voice-activated assistants manage in-car functions such as audio and climate control, offering a seamless, hands-free experience.

Unique capabilities of Toyota's AI

Toyota's AI capabilities are extensive and continuously evolving. Safety Connect remains a foundational feature, using telematics to provide critical safety and convenience features. Additionally, Toyota has developed a machine

---

[22] Ibid

[23] The information in this paragraph, about Toyota's initiatives were sourced from its official newsroom. *Toyota and Generative AI: It's Here, and This is How We're Using It*, Toyota USA Newsroom, September 6, 2023. Available at Toyota's newsroom website: https://pressroom.toyota.com/toyota-and-generative-ai-its-here-and-this-is-how-were-using-it/

learning pipeline to predict low-speed collisions and differentiate them from normal driving events, ensuring better vehicle maintenance and safety.

Predictive maintenance is another area where Toyota's AI excels. By analyzing data from connected vehicles, Toyota can predict maintenance needs for various components, such as batteries, brakes, and tires, before failures occur. This proactive approach ensures more reliable mobility experiences for customers.

AI also powers Destination Assist, a navigation tool that initially relied on human agents. Since May 2023, an automated version of this service has reduced call times and improved efficiency, demonstrating AI's potential to enhance customer service.[24]

How to use Toyota's AI features

Interacting with Toyota's AI features is designed to be straightforward and user-friendly. For instance, the virtual agents "Hey Toyota" and "Hey Lexus" can be activated through voice commands, allowing drivers to control various in-car functions without taking their hands off the wheel. Safety Connect is activated through an SOS button in the vehicle, automatically notifying call center agents in case of a collision.

Benefits from a Total Experience and Total Marketing perspective

AI initiatives significantly enhance customer, employee, and user interactions, as well as multi-experience interactions by delivering efficient, personalized, and innovative services.

- Toyota's AI enhances customer satisfaction by providing proactive safety features and maintenance alerts. The predictive maintenance system ensures that potential issues are identified before they escalate, resulting in a smoother, more reliable driving experience.

- AI-powered features like the virtual agents and automated Destination Assist improve the User Experience by making interactions seamless and intuitive. These tools provide timely assistance, whether it's adjusting the climate control or finding the best route to a destination, all through simple voice commands.

- AI reduces the workload of employees by handling routine tasks, allowing them to focus on more complex and rewarding activities. This shift enhances job satisfaction and productivity, as employees can concentrate on tasks that require human insight and creativity.

---

[24] Ibid.

- Toyota ensures a consistent and integrated experience across various touchpoints, whether customers are interacting with in-car features, mobile apps, or online services. This consistency is key to delivering a cohesive and satisfactory experience for users.

According to Toyota, as of September 2023, AI initiatives have already shown significant results. For instance, the automated Destination Assist service reduced average call times from 102 to 62 seconds and achieved a 92% completion rate. Predictive maintenance models help prevent unexpected breakdowns, improving overall vehicle reliability and customer satisfaction.[25]

Toyota's commitment to AI and generative AI is evident in its continuous investment and innovation, ensuring that these technologies not only enhance current products but also pave the way for future advancements. Thanks to the integration of AI into its core operations, Toyota is setting new standards in the automotive industry, transforming itself into a leader in electrified mobility.

Bibliography

AI-powered convenience: The evolution of Scan & Go, Walmart 2024. Available at: https://tech.walmart.com/content/walmart-global-tech/en_us/blog/post/skip-the-checkout-line-with-scan-and-go-at-sams-club.html

Attard, Monica, Dr Michael Davis, Lisa Main. *Gen AI and Journalism*, UTS, April, 9, 2024.

BofA's Erica Surpasses 2 Billion Interactions, Helping 42 Million Clients Since Launch, Bank of America, April 2024. Available at: BofA's Erica Surpasses 2 Billion Interactions, Helping 42 Million Clients Since Launch | Press Releases | Newsroom | Bank of America.

Bryce, Booth, Jack Donohew, Chris Wlezien, and Winnie Wu. *Generative AI fuels creative physical product design but is no magic wand*, McKinsey, 2024.

Gartner, Peer Connect Perspectives: Robotic Process Automation Use Cases, 2019 (https://www.gartner.com/en/documents/3978927.) This Gartner content is archived and is included for historical context only.

Guenole, Nigel and Sheir Feinzig. *The business case of AI in HR*, IBM, October 2021.

Incandela, Denise. *Walmart Levels Up Virtual Try-On for Apparel With Be Your Own Model Experience*, Walmart, 2022. Available at: https://corporate.walmart.com/news/2022/09/15/walmart-levels-up-virtual-try-on-for-apparel-with-be-your-own-model-experience

Musani, Parvez. *Decking the aisles with data: How Walmart's AI-powered inventory system brightens the holidays*, Walmart Global Tech, October 25, 2023. Available at: https://tech.walmart.com/content/walmart-global-tech/en_us/blog/post/walmarts-ai-powered-inventory-system-brightens-the-holidays.html

---

[25] Ibid.

Sam's Club Begins National Deployment of Automated Inventory Analytics Robots, Walmart, January 27, 2022. Available at: https://corporate.walmart.com/about/samsclub/news/2022/01/27/sams-club-begins-national-deployment-of-automated-inventory-analytics-robots

Talfan Davies, Rhodri. *An update on the BBC's plans for Generative AI (Gen AI) and how we plan to use AI tools responsibly*, BBC, February 28, 2024. Accessible at https://www.bbc.com/mediacentre/articles/2024/update-generative-ai-and-ai-tools-bbc

Toyota and Generative AI: It's Here, and This is How We're Using It, Toyota USA Newsroom, September 6, 2023. Available at Toyota's newsroom website: https://pressroom.toyota.com/toyota-and-generative-ai-its-here-and-this-is-how-were-using-it/

Walmart's Generative AI search puts more time back in customers' hands, Walmart 2024. Available at: https://tech.walmart.com/content/walmart-global-tech/en_us/blog/post/walmarts-generative-ai-search-puts-more-time-back-in-customers-hands.html

Chapter Four
AI & Friends to Boost Total Marketing

Frank Pagano

It's a very exciting time, especially if you are a tech developer. It's a crucial period for human rights, if you are a consumer (a human, in the end) who is acting digitally and physically in a jungle of touchpoints, where every move is recorded, analyzed, and sold back to some entity, from mobile operators to software developers, who, in turn, may come back to you with a proposition, to entertain your eyeballs, influence your behavior and hit your credit card.

Buckle up; there is more technology and applications coming at us, making this whole life much more interesting and stimulating than we dare to imagine.

It's more of a convergence of exponential technologies. Current tech trends, besides AI of course, are the rise of virtual and augmented reality, the so-called internet of behavior (aka *IoB*, which is the interaction of behaviors from hybrid, physical and digital agents), robotics and quantum, not to mention the evolution of all blockchain-based digital and immersive worlds, called metaverses. It would be impossible to run the whole list of applications of these new technologies. We will not do that here.

We will, instead, observe how humans and the world around them will evolve, with a particular deep dive into strategic industries, like healthcare and pharma, energy, and finance. There are obviously monumental implications for data and privacy handling, or for the security of confidential information and the workings of personal incentives for all actors being involved, to make sure the new world is not only plausible, but also profitable and sustainable.

How can companies, of all sizes and industries, adapt to a world where users will be logged in and moving in a context filled with sensors and triggers, agents and new intelligences? How can we take what's coming and use it not to extract value but to build better and better total experiences? Let's start with a bit of theory first, before jumping into real-life cases. Yes, it will be mostly about AI, as we saw from the previous chapter. What else?

4.1. We Need Ownership More Than Creativity

Let's indulge in a daydreaming simulation. Call it: *2030: A Data Odyssey*. It's a random morning in 2030. The head designer's avatar, powered by the latest large language model, has been sifting through all global and local fashion collections, across any brand, plus all the ideas, sketches, social media posts, private conversations, videos, and emails; all of that, since the Roman Empire, thanks to the famous Google Odyssey[1], the world's largest database. The designer is looking for that new idea for a summer shirt, which needs to click with the community identifying themselves with the famous *Berlin Alpha* wave, but with the twist needed to appeal to the tribe in zip code 10115, close to the old wall. The new design is created instantly by AI, and immediately airdropped to the first 1,000, the lucky ones to win the lottery, out of those who signed up for the brand workshop, and they did that with a snap of the fingers of their avatars. With the limited edition, they also receive a fraction of a bitcoin for their ambassadorship. If they generate enough interactions, or 'cool' buzz, on Roblox, only ten shirts will be produced and shipped to their door, to the best-performing jungle influencers. The brand designer did not manually draw anything yet, and her job is rather to interact with fans digitally. Once 'a' design is picked for production, by her, and distributed in a limited-edition physical drop, plus created *en masse* digitally, intellectual property rights and revenues are wired to fans and shareholders instantly, via blockchain, with the most exact calculations processed by quantum computers operating on people's glasses, wearables, or chips installed on their necks. Welcome to the future of fashion. 'Let's create' will soon be replaced by 'let's ask AI'.

We live in a marketing depression phase. "AI will kill creativity and property rights." This is the most common adage, which I hear repeatedly. Guess what? We are not creative as adults and professionals. Most of the stuff that we write online is not original enough to require IP protection. The truth is, we don't even need 'genius' material to succeed in business, as much as we need differentiation and perfect execution. When we see genius or make something extraordinary for one of our brands, we should protect it, because it's risky and transformational, no matter who (or what) does that. To be clear, "to protect" equals "to pay" for it, dearly.

In his latest work, *The Cost of Dull*,[2]Adam Morgan shows how an ad featuring paint drying up performs much better than 85% of all ads out there. The same applies to a video of cows eating grass. Morgan tested his hypothesis quantitatively and presented his insights at the world-renowned Cannes Festival of Advertising (2024), where the most creative people on the planet gather to talk about creativity and drink rosé.

---

[1] This is, obviously, a fantasy name, invented by the authors, just to make sure nobody remains disappointed if they google, indeed, the term. We are daydreaming, as mentioned.

[2] The Cost of Dull is a podcast series, created by the bright, witty, and always entertaining Adam Morgan. More information on: www.thechallengerproject.com.

The issue is that gifted creators are not getting paid. Most interactions on social media are passive (liking stuff), and content tends to be non-original (reposts or retweets). Those who 'create' something new are not getting enough to make a living out of it. According to the Wall Street Journal, 48% of creator-earners made $15,000 or less last year, while just 13% of them made $100,000 or more[3].

The ability of AI, and other exponential technologies, to multiply creative experimentation will give us tools to boost our chances to engage with an audience, if we have something to say (or prompt). What we really need is a system that allows us to track the process and output of AI, while distributing incentives across the food chain. We have the tech stack now.

Will AI disrupt jobs? Yes. Will AI change the way we create? Yes. Will AI change the way we interact digitally? Yes. So, if I run a fashion house, what do I do? Or, better, who am I going to be as a manager, a creator, or a business leader?

Who are you? Creativity is a way of operating, and it needs a business objective. The goal for any business, and society at large, when its powers are augmented by AI and other exponential technologies like blockchain, is threefold:

1. Seek knowledge, like we did since the Enlightenment era (1700s), to solve people's problems, simply and efficiently, and, with inspiration and delight, when we manage VIPs and superfans.

2. Create social capital; namely, make sure that new knowledge and its benefits are shared as widely as possible, rewarding network actions and contributions, in line with people's time and willingness to dance with a brand, via their network of family, friends, and close contacts.

3. Always challenge the status quo, at least digitally (for example, by simulating multiple futures), as technological advances will make any business and profession fragile. AI will help us challenge what it just created, too.

So, keep chasing and running data. AI is the least of your problems. Technology will make us more creative, better suited to identify and reward supporters, and better able to evolve what we do. What will the future look like? Ask AI, but ask the right questions, and check the answers, if you have a vision of what the world could be, know, share and dream. If you are short of ideas, ask AI again. You will not find the 'theory of everything' by 2030. It would be

---

[3] *Social-Media Influencers Aren't Getting Rich — They're Barely Getting By,* The Wall Street Journal, June 17th, 2024.

enough to settle for new knowledge, broad access to it, and the urgency to get ready to change the world.

Now, there is a subtle and dangerous side to the question around machines vs. humans, which comes from the fact that we love the 'work' more than we love the 'workers' behind it. We should discuss how to pay 'genius,' which is the people taking responsibility for a risky move, very often done also with the use of software. Creators do use coding and advanced tech tools today. Are we asking the question because we can contemplate a scenario where we get rid of creative hands or finally can control their rebel heads? Because, deep down, we don't believe creativity has a real impact on hardcore business? Do we really want or need creativity spread all over our org chart? Are we secretly hoping AI will give us better intellectual output, on demand, obedient, and virtually at zero cost?

AI will boost creativity, or at least improve the 'here and now,' which is mostly dull. Genius and risky decisions will remain rare. Creators will survive if we pay them and let them challenge the status quo. They will continue to be the ones able to imagine a different future, inside and outside the company. Creativity shouldn't be afraid of AI. It should fear humans, companies, and boards when they overpay CFOs and CEOs for their average management and sole focus on share price, and it should fear big tech, which will continue to extract value from the world's best work.

4.2. The Price Is Right

"Progress has never been a bargain. You must pay for it. Sometimes I think there's a man who sits behind a counter and says, 'All right, you can have a telephone, but you lose privacy and the charm of distance. (...). Mister, you may conquer the air, but the birds will lose their wonder, and the clouds will smell of gasoline.'"[4]

This is one of the famous sentences of the character Henry Drummond, an atheist and rationalist lawyer, who is the hero of the famous play *Inherit the Wind*, by the American writer Jerome Lawrence. Lawrence's masterpiece, which also became a Hollywood movie starring Spencer Tracy[5], is all about the tension between faith and science, or, as we would say today, between man and technology. In the past, it was human intelligence that dispelled false myths

---

[4] This is one of the latest editions available online: Jerome Lawrence and Robert E. Lee, *Inherit the Wind: The Powerful Drama of the Greatest Courtroom Clash of the Century*, Ballantine Books, 2003.

[5] The movie dates to 1960, while the script was first published in 1955, and it was a success in theaters across the US.

based on religion or on a tired and distorted interpretation of traditions. Today it is the machine, so it seems, in listening to the current debate in the media and social media, that overcomes the limits of human intelligence, to give us a world that is not even imaginable by our minds.

Interestingly, the film, inspired by Lawrence's work, was distributed in Italy as: *And the man created Satan.* What have we done? Is technology the new evil of the world, and will it leave us behind? Will it make us useless? Have machines and science suddenly become the enemy of human intelligence in their unstoppable race? Is the price we are paying or that we will pay too high? Will we bitterly regret what we are giving birth to, as happened to the scientists who invented the atomic bomb?

The contrast with humans is not the right heuristic model with which to approach technology, especially the real phenomenon of recent times, which is AI. Rather, it is a relationship between man and machine, where every exponential technology ends up redefining the way we see ourselves as human beings, inhabit our homes and communities, educate ourselves, work, and love. It is like holding a spring or a rubber band with two hands. Moving one hand has an immediate impact on the other. So, it is all in the tension or balance between humans and technology. That is the right word: balance.

The history of human intelligence has always been a history of efficiency and optimization, of transformation and liberation. Humans have been confronted for millennia with the goal of not only saving physical energy, to devote themselves to more profitable or pleasant tasks, but also of predicting the future more accurately. In the past, the ability to minimize risks was a matter of life and death for families, cities, and entire nations. Today, a greater culture and mastery of data enable companies and communities to increase competitiveness and comfort.

What progress really does is to redefine our identity as individuals and as a community, and hopefully to eliminate inefficiencies and waste. Optimization of available resources becomes the real imperative, considering the current environmental crisis, identified by the World Economic Forum's 2024 report on global risks as the priority for the next decade[6].

The dilemma is atrocious. If we do not progress, we will pay the unacceptable price of an imploding planet. On the other hand, technology without guidelines, in terms of privacy, security and the fundamental laws of the individual, will cost us far too dearly. Until now, we have always paid a price for every step forward. And it was the right one, in the sense that it defined us as contemporary human beings, greatly enriched us and broadened our horizons.

---

[6] *Global Risks Report 2024*, The World Economic Forum (WEF,) January 2024.

The management of the two-year period of COVID-19 showed us the power of progress and the ability of the global community to revolutionize business and human coexistence in a very short period, thanks to the technical prowess of our intellectual capital.

To survive now, we must change, whatever the cost, as long as the price is right. Are we sure that the benefits outweigh the side effects? This is the question everyone must ask themselves. This question lies at the heart of the future of all social and economic activity.

4.3. A Smarter World

Artificial Intelligence, especially in its generative component, which is so much talked about today (see Chapter 3), is widely referred to as a Copernican revolution in our way of operating and existing. Bill Gates, for example, compared it to the invention of electricity. Most CEOs, internationally, point to it as the exponential technology to bet on over the next five years. Alphabet, the holding company of Google and YouTube, and Microsoft have started a long-distance war on AI.

There is no shortage of doubts, fears and risks. Historian Yuval Harari is critical of tools such as ChatGPT and LLMs, or Large Language Models, which are the foundations of the latest developments in Artificial Intelligence[7]. The father of modern AI, Geoffrey Hinton, the known scientist and university professor who resigned from Google, said he was very concerned about the effect that generative AI could have on controlling the narrative of our history, on a global scale, for instance, during key elections or wars, large and small.[8]

It is an exceptional time, ours, and it is essential to define rules of engagement and limits before it is too late. We do not want to downplay the weight of the questions that need to be asked in the face of AI. There is so much work to be done. In fact, this is precisely the time to question ourselves, to set basic guidelines of conduct for the application of new technologies, and to set the right price for change.

Artificial Intelligence, and here I simplify, is nothing but a series of algorithms, which systematize and automate the response to all future eventualities,

---

[7] If we have to pick one publication from Professor Harari, we will choose this one: *Nexus, A Brief History of Information Networks from the Stone Age to AI*, Random House Inc., 2024.

[8] There are plenty of interviews and videos, where both Harari and Hinton discuss their concerns regarding AI. A simple search online will serve you multiple talks and articles. For example, for Hinton, see: https://www.newyorker.com/magazine/2023/11/20/geoffrey-hinton-profile-ai, which is from the authoritative *The New Yorker*.

working on a series of past data and inputs. An ancient technology, if you will, born in parallel with the computer itself, but which is experiencing its own hype. Artificial Intelligence provides a plausible interpretation of things, with a speed of analysis of available data that is infinitely faster vs. humans. AI is a formidable predictive tool and an imperative for any company.

This book is, as you have seen so far, written with a B2B slant, i.e., for companies especially, and focuses on concrete cases of Artificial Intelligence and exponential technologies applied to business, and on the need to refine the data strategy, alongside the adoption of technological tools with which to execute it. The key question is to have a human strategy, along with a machine's, to lump everything digital under it.

Technological progress redefines who we are and what we do, as humanity and as businesses. While doing business is increasingly becoming an exact science, we must not forget the need to have clear values, methods and objectives in producing a unique service to our consumers. This is, and always has been, the true art of success. The good news is that we now have tools, which should make us exponentially better at what we already know how to do, i.e., create value for people, for the environment and for companies. Every enterprise has a protocol for risk management. AI must contemplate one, alongside the strategy of its adoption and its implementation at scale. We will most likely have dynamic, constantly changing plans. Planning, sharing, learning from mistakes, then re-planning, and adjusting the course of action are all skills we have learnt in more than half a century. So, what changes from the past?

4.4. The Luxury of Time and Space

Since the end of World War II and the explosion of capitalism, we have been educated to a progressive dialogue with the consumer, the so-called consumer journey, where brand identity is developed along a necessary time dimension, where marketing kicks in, and along a physical component, where trade, or the brick-and-mortar shops, operate, which still remains the dominant formula for selling something. Furthermore, personalization has been a key growth driver for any brand. The dream of every marketer is to give everyone exactly what they need, at the right time and in the right place.

Today's business is progressive, a hybrid between physical and digital, and increasingly personalized, based on archetypes such as personas, consumer clusters, VIP clubs, and so on. Tomorrow's business will be totally different: instant, digital, and respectful of everyone's punctual journey, ideally without exception to the system's codified rules, which know, even better than we do, how to optimize our interaction with everyday challenges, from traffic to bureaucracy, from education to medical care.

The structural approach to doing business is changing, causing us, as professionals and as citizens of the world, to think of time and space as scarce resources, and to act as if we were a luxury enterprise. There is good news: We finally have the tools to realize the old Mad Men's dream of reaching people's hearts and hitting the mark, going straight to their intimacy, to create brand love or loyalty.

We must be clear. Time and space are not to be canceled. It is not a question of zero waiting time for any service or product, or of delivering everything and everywhere in less than ten minutes, but of automating all those stages of the consumer journey that bring no added value. And this requires a mindset of speed and acceleration, to focus all the company's resources on high-quality, if not memorable, experiences, from pre-purchase, to purchase to after-sale.

Secondly, it is not a matter of eliminating the presence of the physical shop or of selling only on e-commerce, but of putting the entire corporate infrastructure at the service of the digital-first consumer journey, which the new generations will always start from, and which is bigger than the four walls of a brand. Omnichannel gives way to omni-compatibility with the digital lifestyle that the new generations already have.

People have a life beyond the brand. Which does not mean abandoning, as of tomorrow morning, Oxford Street for Discord, or completely moving the entire customer base into the metaverse. Rather, it means envisaging that each brand location, even if the interaction is through wholesalers or an intermediary, has the intelligence to recognize the consumer exactly, physically and digitally, without interrupting them, and anticipating how the brand can be useful to them, in their lives and in that moment. Until now, we did not have the technology to do all this, even if we wanted to. The brand of tomorrow is able, thanks to technology, to eliminate all the unnecessary time and space, to deliver essential and exceptional services. This judicious management of products and services will be governed by data. At this point, we need to ask: Will all markets be commoditized? How to stand out in a world where everything is governed by AI?

4.5. Time and Space for Creativity

According to the essayist Daniel Gilbert, in his famous book *Stumbling on Happiness*,[9] human beings are the only animals that can think about the future and imagine a future other than the one that history, or the data of the past, if

---

[9] Daniel Gilbert, *Stumbling on Happiness*, Vintage, 2007.

we want to use a term more akin to business, has offered them. This tension towards something that does not exist is at the basis of being an enterprise, and, ultimately, of technological progress. It is the same tension that fuels our desire for affirmation and integration, and therefore, to live.

In a fully efficient and rational world, where every second and everywhere falls within a precise strategy of optimizing available resources, the primordial task of humans and any community does not change.

The list of things still to be done is very long. We have important games to play, from broad access to finance, to education, and to healthcare for all. We have a planet to reinvent and save. We have a path of integration and equality of gender, race, creed, and culture. Business must play its role in rethinking our whole world.

What will we do when exponential technologies free us from two-thirds of our occupations, as the American investment bank Goldman Sachs predicts[10]? The answer is simple, and it is not just selling stuff. Or rather, not only. We must go back to doing something that is profoundly human, which is to imagine a different tomorrow than our yesterday, which sickened the earth and did not make us equal. We do not know what the relationship between humans and technology will be in five or ten years' time. Any technology that takes us away from creating a future different from today is not useful. We need breakthrough technologies, sooner rather than later. The price to pay will be right if it facilitates our imagination. Now is the time to define the rules of the game for businesses and communities, so that people's privacy and freedom of choice are not annihilated.

Technology helps us to delegate the dull and the dangerous to machines, so that we can have all the time and space to continue to change, using data, and to imagine a future in sharp discontinuity with the distortions and injustices that the hard facts of today and yesterday tell. Will we be able to do this? Yes, because we are human.

The manager of tomorrow must perhaps be or become more and more of an entrepreneur. Freed from unnecessary tasks and duties, the entrepreneur uses the semantics revealed by technology to give new meaning to the products and services of a market, reimagining trade, finance, education, health, energy, and mobility. We are optimistic about technology when it allows us to evolve, at the right price. We share Professor Howard Stevenson's (Harvard Business School) definition of an entrepreneur, when he says that we must look for opportunities "beyond resources controlled." Tech is simply expanding the scope of information available to us, quickly and at a much lower cost than before. The

---

[10] *Generative AI could raise global GDP by 7%*, Goldman Sachs, April 2023.

homework is to continue to imagine new horizons and opportunities. The brand, which manages to govern its data to design, in an intelligent and informed way, new working models and higher service levels, will win. However, it must do so as quickly as possible, aided by these powerful tools.

4.6. So What?

At this point, especially the CEO or the owner of an SME, might think that all the above is a bunch of beautiful words. A more pragmatic question must be answered: So, what exactly do I do now, and not in five years' time?

There are two components to an intelligence plan (hopefully, it's also an intelligent plan) that go hand in hand. Both rhyme with acting.

1. First, those tech tools that act on the back end of the company, from logistics to supply chain, accounting, suppliers' management, and internal processes, must be adopted, and that leads to the streamlining of the way any product or service is created. If AI does not free up resources between the topline and the operating margin of the profit and loss account of a firm, it is just a cost that nobody needs.

2. Secondly, we need to automate all those components of the company's promotional and communication effort, to remove as many obstacles as possible, time and space above all, between brand and consumer. For example, what are the use cases where a supplier, agency, or consumer can benefit from interacting with a bot, instead of a human, in terms of accuracy, personalization, and speed? If I am a fashion or logistics company, can I provide useful information to my style department or my truck fleet, at the right instant, to have a smooth and flawless creative process or delivery flow? The answer is yes, and all this part will be delegated to the machines.

What the entrepreneur or manager must do at this point is to prevent their core business from becoming a commodity. The CEO must think about where and how to place a unique human touch in the internal and external dynamics of the company. The more the company immunizes itself with the tech vaccine, the more the manager must seek out those human experiences that can be foundational and formative for the dense network of fans, suppliers or consumers. The voice of the brand may be mechanical, for example, in a large part of customer service. That voice, on the other hand, must be human, almost familiar, in dealing with customers who fall into its top one percent.

The more the company becomes automated, the more its managers must focus on data, their own values and the collective wisdom of the market and industry organizations, to correct the inevitable externalities and distortions of the system. While the machine solves concrete, and often tedious, problems in consumers' lives, the manager inspires, surprises and entertains the customer with extraordinary products or services. Today, in light of the revolutions brought about by AI and the advent of Electric Vehicles, most CEOs from the automotive industry see their companies as collectives that solve mobility problems with a wide variety of business models, with the aim of becoming software companies as well, to physically and digitally serve their fans.[11]

AI allows us to delegate many decisions to the machine, shrinking the time and space that separates our consumers from an excellent service. AI brings the company closer to the most intimate part of people than ever before. Data reveals the humanity of people, their wants, their weaknesses, and their desires. The company must find the time and space not to delegate a fundamental decision, i.e., to use that intimacy for something more than making a profit, which remains legitimate. The question for the managers and CEOs of the future is whether they want to use technology and data only to make people love their brands, or maybe to serve these same people, with full respect for their vulnerability and rights, for a long-term vision and horizon. This is a path made of integrity, respect, and collaboration.

This book is dedicated to human and artificial intelligence. And it is dedicated to the manager of the future, who knows the history of technology and why it has come down to us in the way we see it today; who puts together a detailed plan of how to structure business processes, organization and culture, protecting the rights of the people who work in the company and of those who benefit from its products and services; that keeps abreast of concrete application examples, in its own and neighboring markets, with the aim of creating efficiency and impact on the basis of descriptive, predictive and prescriptive tools; and that, finally, is not afraid to continually upgrade its infrastructure and workforce in order to fully exploit the new profit channels, which are freed up or created by tech, without panicking about the neo-luddism of the media and social media. In a nutshell, the mastery of data and full control of the new intelligence factory is the secret of progress, so as not to let the bitter aftertaste of new discoveries surprise, intimidate, and, in the end, block the development of the corporate community.

We believe that the machine is only as evil or benevolent as the hand that drives it. Those who forget the humanity of what we do as a business, as the playwright Lawrence says, will *Inherit the Wind*.

---

[11] To pick one turnaround or transformation case in the automotive industry, which made the news very often, one can study Mr. Luca De Meo's *Renaulution* multi-year transformation plan, launched in 2021. For more information, see: https://www.renault group.com/en/group/our-strategy/.

4.7. Smooth Talkers

Humans have the power to imagine a different future, as mentioned. What we should do, then, is to imagine future scenarios, to be ready for change and to fully enjoy the benefits that are given to those who are aware of them first and move quickly, with new products, services, processes and corporate culture.

The world of the future will live in a tension, or rather in a balance, between two poles:

1. A 'talking' product, i.e., a product always accompanied by its digital twin. The digital twin, to put it another way, of any object or service contains technical and legal specifications, indispensable in the future to sell anything, for example from the US to South Korea, or to guarantee its authenticity (think about the size of the counterfeiting market and of the amount of money that could be given back to creators and right holders); it will also include rewards or personalized offers proportional to the actual engagement of each fan. The digital twin, or digital product passport (DPP), is unique, and it can even be dynamic, thanks to the use of artificial intelligence, which instantly codes and drops into the DPP a proposal calibrated to the person, based on their history, specifically shared by the user to receive unique perks, ideally not purchasable in any other way. Artificial intelligence, which in this case acts as the brain of the interaction with people, is the enabler of a great exodus from a marketing based on a limited set of personas to one that is truly one-to-one, instantaneous and highly accurate. The talking and interactive product is very efficient in its execution. The DPP would not be possible without blockchain, which is a public, transparent, and unassailable register where all interactions between brands and fans are digitally recorded. The correctness of the word spoken to a user is entrusted to artificial intelligence, especially in its generative component, which perfectly interprets all the consumer's signals, in whatever way they are expressed, to provide a plausible and relevant response for each specific case. AI is the fuel of an intelligent engine, capable of speaking to the right person, at the right time and with the right content. Everything is clear, at least on paper. The question now is: Who do I really have in front of me? Who are you, consumer? Do I know you? How can I penetrate your heart and know your desires, so that I can talk to you?

2. A 'talking' consumer, in fact, is what we need to eliminate any inefficiency in the sales ritual and guarantee to those in front of us the service that they deserve. But how can we be sure if the only way to

identify a person today is through an email address, or an SMS, as in the case of the US, or through interaction with a native app, as it often happens in China? How do I know for sure that I'm not selling a bottle of Jack Daniel's, or something worse, to a child? Today, I rely on his or her confirmation click (placing the entire responsibility on the fan), or on a loyalty card, or on database verification, which may not be shared between Dubai, Beijing, Sao Paulo, and New York, or between mono-brand retail, wholesale, franchises, and distributors. The world of the future, whether offline or online, involves the presence of sensors scattered along the consumer journey and worn by people along the funnel itself. This scenario is entirely in line with the philosophy of Apple's latest headset, the Vision Pro, and of spatial computing, which allow the individual, when he or she wants, to (1) be identified immediately thanks to his or her biometric data, which is unique; and to (2) eliminate the risk of missteps and frauds for the brand, which accurately and appropriately rewards the right consumer. It may seem like science fiction, but it is not a future so distant from us. For example, the use of facial recognition is the mechanism that allows us to activate our iPhone and is based on our biometric data. What will happen tomorrow is a roll-out, far and wide, of these tools, which are positioned as a bridge between the physical and digital world (which is precisely the intention of spatial computing), and which will act as a guarantor of identity and status of a fan, who no longer needs the intermediation of the brand to be recognized, especially when traveling between markets and sales channels, offline and online. In addition to a talking product, we will have talking shops and shelves, which instantly recognize talking VIPs, to serve them properly, without unnecessary interludes and checks, with immersive experiences (if we want, finally an evolved metaverse, anchored to reality), which will be relevant and thoughtful, just for him or her. The human touch, to put it in a refined way, intervenes to delight, surprise, and inspire, selectively and only where needed.

The dialogue between product and fans has been mediated by the marketing and sales department, at least until today. The advent of blockchain, digital twins, AI and spatial computing reduces the space and time between the right product and the right consumer, freeing enormous resources, which today are trapped in checks, bureaucracy, verifications, and inefficient promotional practices. The optimization of the sales ritual, especially in a physical store, is not only a formidable liberator of resources, which are essential for the survival of retail itself, but it is the driving force that allows the sales or marketing staff to concentrate on the essence of branding, that is, providing a quality experience and content that is always relevant and captivating. And here AI can help, both in the value creation and in the content creation phases. The generative part of AI, with its large language models, allows us to produce quality messages with a strong innovative capital, within a fraction of a second. Yes, AI will make us more creative, as we said.

This augmented, talking world is still in its hype phase. According to the Economist, not even 2% of American companies use Generative AI in their processes, and spatial computing will see a slow diffusion, also due to the high costs in this initial phase of life.[12]

The priority for any business is to think about the fundamentals first, with an eye always looking at the future. A signature experience, both today and tomorrow, revolves around the enrichment of the product, the channel, and the consumer data to create a community of brand lovers in a timely, efficient, and effective way.

While waiting for the advent of blockchain, artificial intelligence, and spatial computing, a proprietary and distinctive experience always needs some technology. We are talking about technologies that are twenty years old or more, are always current and represent the basis for serving our fans in the best possible way. If we think of Amazon, which has made data and customer obsession its crusade, there are no exponential technologies in sight; yet the delivery giant has managed to create the gold standard of commerce.

Amazon is more the exception than the rule. In today's world, for example, only 25% of business processes travel on the cloud. The UK still imports floppy disks and music cassettes. Twenty percent of companies in the world do not have a website. Most supply chain flows are still managed on Microsoft Excel, if not manually. Cash is still the dominant form of payment globally. Many luxury brands had never done e-commerce before the pandemic. Technological development always occurs slowly, as happened with the spread of electricity and automobiles.[13]

A Total Marketing experience starts from the person and tries to reconstruct and enrich the data around the user, across all contact points and sales channels. For this reason, it is necessary to ensure that the online and offline management systems are connected to each other, as well as equipping oneself with the ability to read the data correctly, to satisfy the customer and increase turnover. A data lake managed via the Cloud, i.e., on servers that are accessible to all players in the network and where all information flows are aggregated,

---

[12] See: *Your employer is (probably) unprepared for artificial intelligence*, The Economist, July 16th, 2023.

[13] Ibid.

cleaned and displayed for management in a simple way, becomes a must for any company that wants to prepare for the future.

Within five years from now, we must have measured and measurable supply and commercial chains, to create that 'talking' product needed by the fan of tomorrow. In addition to a customer data platform (CDP), we need to start developing a sophisticated CRM, trying to segment and delight each sub-target with calibrated and relevant proposals. These technologies, from CDP to CRM packages, are all available, affordable and scalable quickly. These cloud-based marketing, e-commerce and loyalty models today represent 98% of any brand's Customer Experience, and are the natural starting point, or the basics. The suggestion to the CEO reading this book is, therefore, to start from the basics, as we wait for exponential technologies to increase their natural penetration. Total Marketing is less of a marketing theory and more of a concrete manual on how to enhance and use data and put it at the service of business and its entire network of players.

Let's look at some cases from our most strategic industries to have a taste of what the future could look like, and, hopefully, to be of inspiration and reassurance to all leaders out there, in the private and public spheres, who want to start their digital transformation journey.

4.8. Digital Identity

Who are you, Dear Consumer? The best example of innovation in the digital identity arena comes, to my knowledge, from a Swiss startup called Procivis[14], whose co-founder Giorgio Zinetti helps us understand where we stand in the journey towards a 'talking' individual.

Procivis has products and services in the market (differently from many startups who declare to be in their "pre-revenues" phase), especially catering to the public, namely B2C, like in the case of the small town of Zug, Switzerland. Some three years ago, they got bought by a conglomerate that is in the publishing and printing business, going from books to passports.[15]

Procivis created a mobile government platform – in the shape of a native app to be clear, available on smartphones, which contains all personal documents, and which allows users to interact with governmental bodies seamlessly, with services that range from tax payments to the request of documentation needed for work or personal reasons. The identity verification, at every transaction or

---

[14] For more information, see www.procivis.ch.

[15] The buying company is called Orell Füssli Holding AG, which is an interesting case to study, having a business spanning from books to the printing of the Swiss currencies, to passports and now digital identities.

interaction, takes place via an encrypted signature or key, and the experience is always fluid and secure. The digital identity can be utilized in the physical and digital world, and use cases of interoperability with insurance or mobile phone companies have been realized already.

In a nutshell, the identity is verified at first from a public authority, and the encryption of its confirmation empowers the individual to move through public and private services, unlocking efficiencies in the government (freeing up people's time) and increasing the return on taxpayers' money.

> The next step, which is at the stage of a proof of concept, tested with selected enterprises, is the case of a fully decentralized identity, with blockchain serving as the enabler, in the future, of full ownership of one's own data and payments via cryptocurrencies and compensation for personal data utilization, says Zinetti[16].

We are not at the stage where the world recognizes us via our biometric features – at least not in all key jurisdictions globally[17], as that entails a thicker layer of privacy regulations, and which is probably farther from us, but it's a good first step in the direction of eliminating noise and frauds in defining who's who, in front of a public official or a store sales associate, who sells Louis Vuitton bags.

The efficiencies are obvious, and this governmental solution could become the generator of a stream of cash for the state (for example, if sold as a white label product to private enterprises).

"At an international level, we need to work on regulations and compatibility across all national systems, so that we can apply to business and digital identities what happens to our passports when we travel," concludes Zinetti[18].

Switzerland is probably one of the most advanced countries in terms of openness towards blockchain and public tests with technology, but the Procivis example shows us that the tech solution is there. We need to build the legal and trust framework for it to work for business and across nations.

---

[16] Zinetti, Giorgio, co-founder at Procivis and CTO at Cardano. Interview with Frank Pagano. 08/21/2024. Zurich.

[17] We could argue that there are cases, where biometric checks on a nation's population, in public spaces, are deployed widely, like in the UAE.

[18] Zinetti, Giorgio, co-founder at Procivis and CTO at Cardano. Interview with Frank Pagano. 08/21/2024. Zurich.

Dr. Valentino Megale is the co-founder and CEO of Softcare Studios[19], a startup working in the field of virtual reality applied to the health sector. He is also a professor, author and advisor. Megale has the right expertise to add to our discussion on the future of identity. Biometric data will be key to fully unlock physical and digital agency. Eye, voice, and fingerprints are all unique, so we can use them to identify each one of us. Technically, we could do it immediately. The caveat is that data capture always multiplies the chances to expose personal information to potential data breaches, making the stolen data available to malicious stakeholders for fake identity creation, set-up of unconsented bank accounts and online profiles, or extortion. In the digital space, the hacking risk is still sizable.

If we take healthcare, which is the industry where Softcare Studios operates, most institutions are vulnerable by design, as they store vast amounts of sensitive patients' data in centralized systems, often relying on outdated technology that lacks robust security measures. This vulnerability is compounded by limited resources, which prioritize patient care over cybersecurity investments, and insufficient staff training in cybersecurity best practices, making these organizations prime targets for cybercriminals.

Plus, there is a need for more coordinated regulations and interoperability across markets, exactly like Zinetti mentioned. "For sure, at some point AI could recognize what's human or not, what's fake or not, who's who basically, but the risk is there, especially in all contexts where the tech stack is obsolete," confirms Megale[20].

A step, explored in certain contexts, is to implant a chip into our bodies, which is something that companies like Neuralink are initiating. Invasiveness allows us to collect tons of data, and the watch-out remains the same, namely, the temptation for data owners to misuse the information, or for malicious actors to hack the systems.

Another example, according to Megale, is the Meta[21] Ray-Ban glasses, which represent a transitional technology, namely wearable devices that capture data both from users and their surroundings. This introduces significant risks and novel surface attacks. Similarly, technologies like Neuralink, which interpret brain waves, could also be vulnerable to hacking, not only as data-reading devices but also as writing ones, able to impact brain activity digitally.

---

[19] For more information, see www.softcarestudios.com.

[20] Megale, Dr. Valentino, co-founder and CEO at Softcare Studios. Interview with Frank Pagano. 08/24/2024. Zurich.

[21] Meta as the group Meta, the owner of Facebook, Instagram, Threads and WhatsApp.

At a public and private level, work needs to happen to start defining a consistency of standards for identities. This is going to be extremely useful, also and especially for companies.

Megale also weighs in on the ownership of own data.

> It's feasible, but are we ready to manage the responsibility of being in charge? Are we ready to own our private keys and have total control on our data? Do we really have the culture to manage our most delicate data, with no intermediaries? There are examples out there for clinical trials. In companies such as Aimedis,[22] participation in a trial is recognized with a NFT, containing credits, which the user can spend at their convenience. Technically, we can. The question is if we have the culture and the right legal framework to jump ahead and roll this out, he states[23].

From a technological point of view, digital identities, decentralized or semi-decentralized, are feasible. The technology, which is a mix of blockchain, AI and biometrics, is there. We need to understand if we can put together a business model and have the culture and trust to live in a system that is automated, even for the most personal and intimate decisions, like paying taxes or voting for our governments. The quality of the data becomes essential, and even OpenAI is starting to be willing to pay for it.

Megale makes the example of Perplexity and OpenAI, which are now doing partnerships with media and publishers, to get their (official) hands on quality content for AI to train on. But the problem is: our productivity-obsessed culture values speed more than proper due diligence and responsible innovation. This increases the gaps between regulation efforts and the rapid and unpredictable rise of new financial monopolies, based on data and artificial intelligence. What's urgent on our to-do list, in light of this tension between privacy and fast capital gains, is cultural readiness and ethical consensus on rules, across the world's regions.

Who are you? You might ask when you see a new face in your store. You will know in a split second, safely and with zero risk of fraud. We can know, we can pay for your data, and we can give you ownership. We need to agree on standards and rules to keep the bad guys at bay, including big tech selling my most precious assets, namely the million slices of my personal life.[24]

---

[22] For more information, see: www.aimedis.com.

[23] Megale, Dr. Valentino, co-founder and CEO at Softcare Studios. Interview with Frank Pagano. 08/24/2024. Zurich.

[24] At a macro-level, a future-proof digital ID solution, scalable and accessible, will tackle another huge inefficiency. According to the World Economic Forum (WEF) there are 850

4.9. If These Walls Could Talk

Our spaces will not talk. They will scream, mass-produce data and turn into big, smart wonder boxes. Squares, streets, stores, hospitals, schools, offices, and so forth, will be populated with AI-powered sensors and augmented reality features, which will be able to act, react and proactively serve what we need, instantly and *in toto*. Everything will be tracked, in full respect of local regulations, so that data will flow where needed, to make sure business or social objectives are met; getting a passport or buying furniture will be as simple as ordering a cappuccino at Starbucks.

You may not believe me. This is why we cross-checked our predictions with Andrea Abrams, Founder and CEO at Phygicode[25], advisor, investor, and board member. Abrams is a technology veteran with a rich background in real estate and retail. She is based in the US, but has clients everywhere in the world, as the "phygital revolution," as she calls it, is something that affects us all.

In the 1990s, before the expansion of e-commerce, the retail industry consisted of thousands of brands and product sellers, but only a handful of truly exceptional retail operators. Many of these operators managed to remain relevant by expanding geographic reach with digital commerce, increasing experiential in-store connections, and eventually building stronger loyalty with social media platforms. They remained true to their DNA and took their community through the transition. In some cases, their products changed, and the channels of distribution improved, but the relationship with the customer evolved to a more community-oriented engagement.

"Operators of retail experiences today must understand that we live in the era of intersectional culture, and the product is a connector. The product is part of a service. Access, culture and community are the foundations," Abrams states[26].

We are moving into a hybrid future, where digital and physical will merge, work together, and be in an ever-moving balance, to surround humans and serve them at best. According to Abrams, the present is phygital, as we chase access instead of possession. Culture and community become the true priorities, over possession and self-affirmation.

Doing business in physical retail some thirty years ago was tough, if you wanted to make sense of it, as many Gen X professionals may recall. For

---

Mil people who still lack legal ID, and are therefore unable to engage with society. Another huge value pool, which can be activated via technology. For more information, see: *Reimagining Digital ID*, The World Economic Forum, June 2023.

[25] For more information, see www.phygicode.io.

[26] Abrams, Andrea, Founder and CEO at Phygicode. Interview with Frank Pagano. 08/10/2024. Zurich.

example, shopping malls had sales assistants going around with Palm Pilots (the ancestors of iPad, for younger readers), asking five questions to all shoppers, from what they bought to why, from pricing to satisfaction. Data would be collected and processed by external agencies, who would brief mall owners and operators on how to improve their services. The whole thing was cumbersome, inaccurate, slow, and rarely insightful.

It's a different era now. The context around us will be able to track what people do, using wearable technologies and sensors spread around us. Data will flow into AI-powered engines, able to make sense of it, predict and suggest, with the goal to simplify, inspire, and delight our fans.

According to Abrams, the world will move along three avenues:

- Connected experiences: Every product will be connected and have a digital twin; this is already happening, from fashion and luxury to the industrial world.

- Phygital environments: This will take a bit more time; thanks especially to augmented reality, digital and physical will interact to guide fans, to lead them through games, treasure hunts, discoveries, and so forth; phygital is a language, a code that every brand is going to use to engage users and build loyalty; sports is a great example of this, but business and government will greatly benefit from these new capabilities.

- Data capture: This is where AI will play its pivotal role, feeding recommendations and real-time propositions to every human immersed in this phygital universe.

There is, of course, room for blockchains in Abrams' vision.

"Blockchain will lead to better adoption of new solutions. On-chain activities force us to operate with 'truth' instead of 'trust,' and this will be crucial, as we enter an era that will highly value authenticity more than ever before," concludes Abrams[27].

There is a continuous loop that embraces fans in phygital marketing. Physical leads to digital, and vice versa. The gaming world understands this. Games need to be powered by strong communities and great experiences that are phygital. Pudgy Penguins,[28] for example, is a web3 project that went mainstream through their retail partnerships with Walmart and Target, and now they are

---

[27] Ibid.

[28] For those who missed the craze around Pudgy Penguins, it's an NFT collection - yes, launched during the 2021 hype, and based on the Ethereum blockchain. For more information, see www.pudgypenguins.com.

combining their efforts by building a game with Mythical on the Mythical Platform and Mythos Chain, already used by millions of consumers.

"Shopping leads to access to a community and culture. Communities merge, fans share their experiences, leveraging the brand values, being rewarded for their engagement and receiving social status for their participation," says Abrams[29].

Technology gives operators, brands, governments, and corporations the tools to nurture communities, but it forces them to fireproof the intent of everything they do, the reason why they exist in the first place.

"We see a lot of deductive narrative, copy - paste, which is old school. Brands need to be authentic and have a long-term plan, when it comes to managing communities. It all starts with company culture and mindset," warns Abrams[30].

Welcome to the era of data, truth and authenticity. If done well, human connections will be heightened by technology. Technology is one piece of a puzzle made of space for fans to create, hardware and AI tools that track and interact, and infrastructure that is interoperable and so smooth that it becomes invisible.

Walls will talk, so that we can, as humans, talk to each other better, deeper, faster. If the present is phygital, our future can be even more human.

4.10. The Kids are Alright

The future of healthcare is too important. We need broader access and cheaper utilization of the current infrastructure.

Valentino Megale, co-founder and CEO at Softcare Studios [31], helps us understand how to solve for access and cost. They don't collect data about patients, by choice, even though they could from a technological point of view. [32] In general terms, virtual reality solutions (leveraging headsets, immersive experiences and ad hoc software) collect data, monitor patients from a distance, and de-localize care.

In his view, governments and health institutions could create centers of excellence spread across the nation, with reach executed via digital connections. Today's risk is an overload of hospitals, and the frequent burnout of healthcare employees. So, technically, the solution is there, and technology

---

[29] Abrams, Andrea, Founder and CEO at Phygicode. Interview with Frank Pagano. 08/10/2024. Zurich.

[30] Ibid.

[31] For more information, see: https://www.softcarestudios.com/.

[32] Megale refers here to the stand of Softcare Studios, his company. It's his decision, besides legal obligation, to be very cautious on personal data and information.

could help reduce the pressure on health operators and increase access to quality care and clinical talent, wherever patients are.

Softcare Studios, which provides VR solutions to support patients undergoing surgeries and other invasive procedures (reducing the traditionally associated sedation rate) and practitioners' training, works with selected hospitals and, for now, collects relevant data only via research institutions and universities, which are more regulated and have ethics committees able to oversee these tests.

Softcare uses the same technology for patients and practitioners. They expose patients to virtual worlds during surgeries, making them more relaxed and reducing sedation. Virtual stimuli are adapted to specific target categories of patients and the related medical procedures. Potentially, these experiences could be personalized, crafted *ad personam*, triggering reactions and behaviors useful to infer clinical conditions. Behaviors change if you have a deficit or a condition. Therefore, data could also be predictive of diseases like Parkinson's or Alzheimer's. And, right there, you start to see the subtle line between helping patients and getting access to their most intimate secrets.

The same system, made of headsets, immersive digital worlds and personalized experiences, and powered by AI, can be used for continuous training. One Accenture Park[33] is a clear example of training done efficiently and effectively across hundreds of thousands of employees, who accelerate their performance from the very onboarding to the daily operations. The same goes for PwC, Walmart, Hilton Hotels; the list is infinite. The training for employees is both functional and emotional, as a tech-powered learning system can prepare employees for various experiences, via simulations and finessing of the learning experience that is catered to every individual, in a slightly different fashion.

The same caveat goes for enterprises. Companies will handle data that can be sensitive. This should not be penalizing for the employees, because of its predictive edge, when looking at career opportunities or risk management. The data can be transformed into a marker, leading to people scoring. This is the risk.

The results from the use of virtual reality, hardware and AI are impressive. In the end, if we look at the example of Softcare, virtual sedation does work. A patient usually gets an anesthetic twice. It's a local and total anesthesia. The total anesthetic is avoidable if Softcare's protocol becomes mainstream.

Total anesthetics are administered to protect all stakeholders. It's mainly for comfort and caution. But the impact is more time spent in the surgery room;

---

[33] This is Accenture's "metaverse," so to speak, dedicated to employees and partners. For more information, see: https://www.accenture.com/us-en/about/going-beyond-extend ed-reality.

the specialist anesthesiologist needs to use more time and care for peculiar cases, who could suffer from heavier doses of sedation, and more time to wake up, with potential side effects. Virtual reality is showing to be a good fit for most surgeries, where total sedation is not needed, like for mastectomy, hernia, or vascular access procedures. In just a few tests, the company was able to reach efficiencies worth EUR 0.1 million on kids' surgeries. This shows the potential for savings and impact at scale.

Again, technologically, a new horizon for healthcare is within reach. Access will go up, and costs will move down at exponential rates. Rules, incentives and interoperability of data across hospitals, nations, and regions will be turnkey. What about suppliers? Industries like big pharma, med-tech, or insurance will for sure be interested in having access to this data, when anonymized and cleaned. They would pay for it. The financial balance is easy to find if we get data and can process it fast and right. We will live in a world where patients get less sedation, risk less, and recover faster. We will live in hospitals where clinicians are better trained. The convergence of VR, AR, and AI is expected to reduce risk and mistakes. The kids are alright, in a future run by responsible technology.

What about certified data? What's the role of blockchain in all of this? Can we make sure the process and outcome of the data factories that we are creating are transparent and public? And can healthcare be performed by machines, as there is an obvious shortage of humans in the field?

We asked Andrea Biffi, entrepreneur, board member, and advisor in healthcare.

Robots are being used already in healthcare. For example, robots give surgeons relevant information on how to operate, they assist with cutting, they identify areas that they shouldn't touch. AI already powers surgical robots, and the more surgeries, the better the tool and the outcome. The data is used at patient, doctor and supplier level. But, just to be clear, initial signals are positive, and we are at the beginning of a journey, says Biffi[34].

As an example, any endoscopy takes time for execution and assessment by doctors or specialists. AI works differently and better: It will tell you right away the situation, as the instrument is in use, sifting through tons of benchmark data, identifying pathologies, and predicting potential ones.

Robots will assist humans and take most of their tasks, the tedious ones, for example, while reducing noise and mistakes.[35] The outcome is improved for

---

[34] Biffi, Andrea, Independent entrepreneur, board member and advisor. Interview with Frank Pagano. 08/21/2024. Zurich.

[35] The absolute best read on "noise" is, indeed: Daniel Kahneman, Olivier Sibony and Cass R. Sunstein, *Noise: A Flaw in Human Judgment*, Little, Brown Spark, 2021.

patients, but it's the entire network of practitioners and suppliers that can benefit and be interested in having the data.

> We will monitor the real-life use of all medical tools, have insight from data and an informed dialogue with suppliers. Rent systems are already in place for machines and robots, so AI can help us improve procurement and engage suppliers in better innovations, without having to expose ourselves upfront with huge Capex. The data is exposed, and everything is controllable. This has an impact also on the whole network of the insurance business, continues Biffi[36].

We said it many times in these chapters. Technologically, we can solve for better experiences for patients, better data for practitioners and suppliers. Data is there. The next step, according to Biffi and his team, is certified data on blockchain. This is one of the projects that he is working on, as it will have an impact on risk and legal assessments and costs, bringing them down dramatically.

Giovanni Di Napoli is the CEO of Cosmo Pharmaceuticals[37] and he is a veteran in the industry, having worked between the US and Europe for over twenty-five years. He has seen medical devices change exponentially, indeed, thanks to technology.

One of the large corporations he worked for manufactures a capsule *(we will not mention any names, as he left the company)* which is able to take pictures of our internal organs, after being ingested. As he recalls, the data upload to the desktop would take four to five hours, and the physician would spend one hour analyzing everything once downloaded. With the introduction of an AI-based software, a machine can sift through over ten million images to get precious information about the patient. The processing time is reduced to below twenty minutes. Tech dramatically boosts the physician's ability to understand, quickly, the status of any patient.

There are so many other examples of tech applications in the medical field, if you ask Di Napoli. They were able to bring down the time for reading a report by a doctor from one hour to below twenty minutes, as mentioned, and without sacrificing quality. The space occupied by tech devices and recorders would shrink dramatically over time, as is the case when tech comes into play.

Partnerships are also a big success factor in the medical field. They tapped into the expertise of big tech companies from Silicon Valley, such as Google,

---

[36] Biffi, Andrea, Independent entrepreneur, board member and advisor. Interview with Frank Pagano. 08/21/2024. Zurich.

[37] For more information, see: www.cosmopharma.com.

Salesforce, and Apple, using a mix of cloud-based software and AI. Medical devices must be approved by the FDA (in the US[38]) which require lots of clinical and regulatory efforts, so it's important to have a diverse stakeholders' pool to succeed.

Plus, one of the big challenges with patients' data is privacy, and this is also true for the US, which is usually not as strict as Europe. In the EU, every country has its own rules, on top of GDPR. This applies even for data collection for mere clinical purposes. Moreover, every institution has a different IT department, with its own needs and standards. "We need guidelines and clarity, urgently," stresses Di Napoli[39].

The urgency comes from the fact that data is the future. Take the case of colonoscopies, for example. AI is a true game changer. This is a real-time exam, and if you don't see something, you can't go back and watch it again. Tech helps doctors detect precancerous lesions with a precision that is shocking. Di Napoli's team improved detection of conditions conducive to cancer by 14% and reduced the miss rate by 50%.

> As a company, we decided to share some of the data, with the proper consent, so that other institutions could benefit from it, and have the same impact, if not more, for their own exams. There is a market for data, but, more than that, I would say that there is a clear win in sharing information and building networks, where tech and cooperation explode and distort the common interest of the public, practitioners and all stakeholders, closes Di Napoli[40].

To reach scale, MedTech companies should manufacture devices with this mindset, so that data sharing is in the DNA of every machine. But we need to change an overly cautious culture, affected by risk aversion and slow reaction time from governments and international organizations.

> I am fine with full ownership of data with people, the patients, and with incentivizing virtuous behaviors with tangible rewards, like a discount on insurance costs, for example. The more data, the better any AI tool will give feedback. Also, from an organizational point of view, pharma and medical companies must make sure IT and tech teams are brought into business discussions. The time when business and tech decisions

---

[38] Di Napoli was in the US with his previous employer.

[39] Di Napoli, Giovanni, CEO at Cosmo Pharmaceuticals. Interview with Frank Pagano. 08/25/2024. Zurich.

[40] Ibid.

were separated is over. We need diverse and cross-functional business teams, working together to achieve results, which benefit the whole network of stakeholders, sometimes with tailor-made approaches, concludes Di Napoli[41].

A radical transformation of a strategic industry, like healthcare, is within reach. This will have an exponential impact on the economy. Data collection starts from hospitals, at the local, regional, and national levels. We need all data, including its variability. AI will make sense of it. Blockchain will certify it. These are the steps to better and more accessible care for all. Our kids will be alright. Do we care to make sure that happens? This is the question, and the answer is to give global care a future.

4.11. AI Teachers, Don't Leave Those Kids Alone

Pooling, cleaning, and making sense of data will make us healthier and will give us longevity. Above all, exponential technologies will broaden access to healthcare, progressively including the entire world population, thanks to new capabilities and dramatically lower costs. The advantages of tech need to be assessed from the margin of the empire, indeed, namely, by how much new tools can liberate those living at the periphery of society. Their data is valuable, and their markets can be unlocked, at least technologically, as we saw in the previous section. There is another immense industry that will be disrupted by a Total Marketing approach, and that's the field of education.

Technology has already entered schools and education, via the format of apps, which open to solutions that resemble social media, like in the case of GoStudent (personalized tutoring, including ratings and reviews for students and teachers) or Education First (with the additional elements of community, travel, and continuous training, across all ages).[42]

There is a lot more that we can do when AI, especially, enters the room. According to the World Economic Forum (WEF), this is a fantastic time to rethink and step up our education system.[43] This is why the WEF calls it

---

[41] Ibid.

[42] For more information, see: www.gostudent.org and www.ef.com. These are two of the most popular digital services of training and education across the globe, just to give a flavor of what current technology can do.

[43] The latest report on the subject is called: *Shaping the Future of Learning: The Role of AI in Education 4.0*, The World Economic Forum, April 2024.

Education 4.0, which rhymes with the other *4.0* labels applied by the institution to the multiple fields of modern stakeholders' capitalism, as they call it.[44]

Besides the obvious impact of AI, especially in its generative component, on efficiency (for example, bureaucratic tasks and grading, just to name two) and on narrowing the global gap of the millions of teachers needed to cater to the global community[45], what is intriguing is (1) the ability provide ultra-personalized teaching and mentoring, also via avatars or bots; (2) a modified and living curriculum, which will cover digital skills and coding, the functioning of AI itself (solving problems like AI would do, breaking them down in pieces and working as a team), plus the hot topics of cybersecurity and data protection; (3) the possibility, in line with the idea of Total Marketing, to pool usage data, continuously, and make sense of them, feeding insights back to students, families, teachers, public institutions, curriculum creators, and so forth, and making the system progressively more efficient and effective. At a regional and international level, more data enables the sharing of best practices faster, and access to education in geographical areas or parts of the population who may be left behind.

From digital textbooks to virtual mentors, from computational thinking to 3D simulators, the pilots illustrated by the WEF in their latest report show increase rates in literacy, higher participation of women in STEM subjects[46], and a more informed dialogue between the actors who are shaping the school system, from Asia to Africa, to Western countries. So far, so good. It does work, it seems.

What's missing is something basic and something extremely ambitious. The basic item is easier to solve: The digital divide is as big as 2.6 billion people without the internet[47]. It is a matter of investments in technical infrastructure. For example, Edison Alliance, a multi-stakeholder non-profit organization, is already working on connecting one billion lives by the end of 2025, via public and private support. The second need is, as mentioned in other chapters of the book, an international alignment on data protection, interaction with AI, and on the definition of how to process and monetize personal data (in this case, especially when we are dealing with under-age students,) so that new value streams can be unlocked, as we integrate AI into the education mix. As human and virtual teachers, we cannot afford to leave our kids alone. We need to protect them from machines and from the secondary agenda of public or private actors, so that they learn how to develop critical thinking, together with

---

[44] Klaus Schwab and Peter Vanham, *Stakeholder Capitalism: A Global Economy that Works for Progress, People and Planet*, Wiley, 2021.

[45] The WEF estimates it's at least 44 million teachers missing globally.

[46] Science, technology, engineering and mathematics.

[47] For more information, see: www.edisonalliance.org.

their functional skills, and to innovate and challenge the status quo, or socialize and develop their communities further, as we distribute the vast economic rewards of *Education 4.0*.

4.12. Make it Rain

Let's talk about the shameful topic of money. We don't like to discuss our finances. They belong to the most intimate spheres of our lives. Taxes or capital gains are not the typical small talk of cocktail parties, and wealth managers behave more like members of a religious sect than a happy bunch of *comrades*. The overall culture of banks is cautious and conservative, as the system is heavily regulated to protect users and the broader public from risks and fraud; so, talking about money wouldn't be fun at any other time of the day. Banks are not big tech companies. They don't have their disruptive spirit, cool factor, and *nonchalance* in trading data.

Massimo Morini, university professor, converted banker and expert in exponential technologies[48], confirms: "the world of finance has always used technology[49]."

For example, algorithms for trading and predicting trends, cloud infrastructure, digital transformation, from apps to world-class consumer journeys, chasing the smoothest online experience at the maximum level of security and privacy. However, it has been historically difficult to revolutionize it. Consumer data has been understood and handled much better in other industries. The heavy regulation and security protocols have, for sure, hindered innovation. Data is the heart of a Total Marketing approach, and banks struggle, by design, to transform customer information into a market and tradable material.

Maybe AI will change things?

> AI is mainly for efficiency purposes, namely, to resolve back-office, middle-office or management issues, releasing resources for higher value-added tasks. It is also useful for regulatory compliance, which means a stronger grip on internal documents and processes. The

---

[48] It would be too long to list all the roles and responsibilities of Mr. Morini. He teaches at Università Bocconi, Politecnico di Milano and Università della Svizzera Italiana (USI,) has worked at The World Bank and Intesa SanPaolo, and is one of the world's most authoritative experts in public blockchains, having worked, for example, as the Chief Economist for the Algorand Foundation.

[49] Morini, Massimo, University Professor and independent advisor. Interview with Frank Pagano. 08/21/2024. Zurich.

approach is, however, siloed. It's hard to predict a dramatic change of behavior, because of the semi-public roles of banks[50].

AI could help front office teams with the creation of content, products, and propositions calibrated to the needs of individual clients, and will make the suppliers' management more fluid, optimizing processes and killing the fat of inefficiencies, because the whole industry is looking for every cent they can get, after the many bank collapses of the early 2020s, especially in the US[51].

New banks and payment systems, like Revolut and Klarna, have killed fees in exchange for personal data. However, their model is more like social media (media platforms for partner brands) than financial institutions or Total Marketing players (data is not pooled and shared outside, by law, if they want to keep their license), and most of these new digital firms did not pass the scrutiny of the authorities. Traditional banks, to be clear, still run most of the world's net worth and current generations, boomers and Gen X-ers, are cool with it. J.P. Morgan is still the biggest US bank, with way more than $3 trillion of assets under management. Traditional banks also dominate the financial landscape in China.

What kind of tech and financial innovation would foster the development of a Total Marketing approach to businesses and communities? Probably easier, cheaper, and faster payments, which would virtually zero the space and time between interactions across fans, manufacturers, and suppliers. For all lovers of crypto, the following statement will be a source of disappointment. The most successful and widespread innovation in payments will not be Bitcoin.

According to Morini, banks are not likely to use public registries and crypto. There are too many uncertainties, like the legal responsibilities of worst-case scenarios and obvious issues linked to customer service. It's simple stuff, like the functioning and the cost of a system governed by a community that sits outside the four walls of the bank or the state.

Banks are waiting to see the move of governments and central banking institutions before making their own. In Morini's view, Central Bank Digital Currencies[52] (CBDC) could help make our world more liquid, and they are being explored across the globe, from Europe to China. They will require a new tech infrastructure, and none of the public blockchains qualify. They will be

---

[50] Ibid.

[51] The bank run and then collapse of the Silicon Valley Bank in 2023, and its contagion to the whole US financial system hit the global media and left a mark in people's minds and pockets internationally.

[52] As an example, see the development of a Digital Euro. For more information, check the European Central bank website: www.ecb.europa.eu.

controlled by regional central banks, guaranteeing trust across markets, while giving easier retail access to liquidity, like a tokenized currency would do, even for the smallest transactions.

To be seen is what roles traditional banks will or could play in this set-up, as the tech would allow the center, in theory, to manage payments without intermediaries.[53] Will central banks be bold enough to use blockchain like all crypto communities? Unlikely.

> They will probably regain some of the monetary power that has belonged to retail banks in recent decades, and they will leave the management of customer relations to them, leveraging their current trust model, while making access to liquidity easier, even for the smallest transactions, concludes Morini[54].

Traditional banks could become providers of services, while regional digital currencies would oil the business and social engines of our economy. This would be in line with data flowing across the food chains, and with newly created markets for data, which would require micro-payments (lower fees), fewer intermediaries and fewer local obstacles. The presence of a central authority would be an easier sell for CBDC to retail users than money subjected to the whims of a community running a decentralized network, even though we can assume interoperability between the best cryptocurrencies and a digital Euro, for example, will happen at some point.

All good, on paper. While technologically this is straightforward, the caveat is always on checks and balances, and on having a voice to monitor and challenge authorities, in case the center is not aligned with the will of the people, who express their say via democratic elections. We can make it rain, technologically at least, but we need umbrellas, in case a summer drizzle turns into a storm.

"There is a trend towards financial centralization, at least in the past 20-25 years or so. Traditional banks will need to transform and become less vulnerable, if they want to be more autonomous from central banks," Morini points out[55].

---

[53] This is probably the best legacy of the blockchain movement: namely access to value for all. Digital, tokenized currencies will be available to all those who have an internet connection and a digital identity (two of the themes mentioned earlier). We could potentially bank the unbanked, who are approximately 1.5 Bil people globally, according to The World Bank. For more information, see: www.worldbank.org.

[54] Morini, Massimo, University Professor and independent advisor. Interview with Frank Pagano. 08/21/2024. Zurich.

[55] Ibid.

Our point of view is that banks will find their way, create new niches, and enjoy the proximity to fans for paid, concierge-like consultations. Business will always be about someone else's money. The era of machines will make payments fit for the open world of Total Marketing. What we need is fireproof rules, so that someone else's money doesn't count more than my vote.

4.13. Walk the Talk

Sweat Economy, the ecosystem that literally grows at every step of each one of its users[56], knows how to build a movement. And the movement, forgive the cheap pun, is based on convincing fans to move.

As we review the case of Sweat, together with its Chief Marketing Officer, Misha Lederman, we have an underlying question in our mind: how do you manage a community and keep it engaged? Most communities and loyalty programs, for example, see most fans as being passive. Most rewards are left unused, building huge liabilities on companies' P&Ls. Fans are, most often than not, locked into a system, which doesn't allow flexibility, customization and agility. For example, this is true for Starbucks' points (called Stars) or American Airlines miles. You can imagine how hard it is to have people join in and comply when it comes to something as boring as a sustainable, positive, and community-friendly behavior, such as walking. Where is my private utility in socially positive actions?

1.8 billion people today are considered inactive, of which 28% are adults. But the shocking number is that 81% of teens are not moving. You can see how health has not penetrated new generations. "We need to act now, if we want our future communities to live longer and more healthily," says Lederman[57].

Sweat has already reached over 200 million people, generating an ecosystem with like-minded fans, partners, and suppliers. The idea came some ten years ago, with a native app, called Sweat Coin[58], which is, we shall say, a web2 app, with 12 million monthly average users (MAU) and over 700 partners offering rewards and incentives in the app. Sweat Economy is the crypto wallet, which goes on top of that community, born a couple of years ago; so, it's totally web3. It has 14 million downloads and 2.5 million MAU, with 70 partners involved.

> We had to wait until the early 2020s, when blockchain tech solutions reached the right level of scalability and throughput, so that managing

---

[56] For more information, see: www.sweateconomy.com.

[57] Lederman, Misha, Chief Marketing Officer at Sweat. Interview with Frank Pagano. 09/15/2024. Zurich.

[58] For more information, see: www.sweatco.in.

transactions could be fast and efficient[59]. The token element adds to the mix a lot more liquidity, giving fans the chance to decide what to do with it, or even to sell it, if the price is right on various public exchanges out there. If you are active, you should be compensated by private and public institutions that value that behavior. Rewards should be sufficiently smart and flexible to adjust to your individual needs, and you need web3 for that[60].

The web2 app has the traditional streams of revenues of similar digital products, namely advertising, partnerships and premium subscriptions. The web3 layer can create a whole economy around steps, adding exchange services, staking, receiving, sending, and selling, just to name a few. Of course, there are partnerships and advertising, but fans' activity creates an economy, which is self-standing and profitable.

How does it work? The tokens are called Sweat, and they are minted as users take steps. Say, from three to ten thousand steps, they mint tokens, which get dropped into members' wallets. Each day, it takes more steps to receive tokens. Tokens can be spent for rewards, or to lower the cost of additional services, can be put aside into staking and pooling programs, used for learning or marketing tasks, or sold for cash (Fiat), and so forth. Fans are free to do whatever they please (which is not the case for the vast majority of loyalty programs) and receive a sort of asset, which can yield a profit, being a token, and has higher liquidity and latitude than your traditional loyalty point.

It's all driven by tangible rewards and freedom to stretch rewards, according to everyone's needs. Movement has a massive impact on our society and our healthcare system, and the only way to move the needle in people's lives is to seriously incentivize positive behavior. Sweat wants to be the first decentralized app to change the lives of one billion people, creating a positive and real economy of change.

We have other features in our roadmap, like a full ownership of data for members, and the data monetization for stakeholders like MedTech and insurance players, but we need the right regulation and context for that to happen. We can for sure unlock more economic value out of people's actions and data. The secret sauce is in the agility, speed and width of the ecosystem. The smart-phone tracking is also paired with a proprietary technology, which zeroes fraud risks, while preserving

---

[59] Sweat uses the Near Foundation Blockchain. For more info, see: www.near.org.

[60] Lederman, Misha, Chief Marketing Officer at Sweat. Interview with Frank Pagano. 09/15/2024. Zurich.

people's privacy. We are serious about health, and created a sustainable scheme, which does good and well for all who join our movement[61].

Are we serious about our most strategic industries, like health, mobility, energy and education? The case of Sweat shows that we can walk the talk, literally, but we need to share rewards generously with the community if we want impact. Tech is there and is ready. We just need to get active, accepting the fact that fans want in and want to get paid. Money needs to walk as fast as people's steps. Rewards should be as liquid as their sweat.

4.14. The Future of Money

One of the most important changes of the past thirty years is the advent of a digital and globalized economy. Thanks to the web, we could finally write and read content generated by random users from all over the planet, on top of the official channels and traditional media. Information was democratized and decentralized.

One piece was missing, though: money. Until companies like PayPal gave the whole internet movement an additional purpose: commerce. Websites switched overnight from branded vitrines to profit and data centers. Trading could be done 24/7, and the world was introduced for the first time to the idea of digital money and to a global marketplace that was increasingly more open and liquid. Total Marketing needs full liquidity of data and money flows. Are we there yet?

In 2023, PayPal introduced its first stable-coin, anchored to the US dollar (called PYUSD [62]), and in 2024, the coin was added to Solana, another blockchain, on top of Ethereum. The coin is available to the US market (as we are writing this), and the move has brought over 300 million wallets on chain and reached more than $1 billion market capitalization within three weeks from launch. While in the old days, you would need to have a bank account to use PayPal (which is, to buy and sell anything online), a blockchain-based currency opens new entry points into the global economy. PYUSD, indeed, is exchangeable with other cryptocurrencies and functions exactly like one. The addition of Solana, which has been designed for high throughput and security, allows PayPal to compete, for example, with the Visa network, head-to-head. Is the financial sector ripe for disruption? Are we going to witness some kind of

---

[61] Ibid.

[62] For more information, see: https://www.paypal.com/us/digital-wallet/manage-mo ney/crypto/pyusd.

Star Wars, where financial giants must defend their kingdoms and fight for brand new territories, unveiled by exponential technologies?

This is why we speak to Tom Rieder, serial entrepreneur and Managing Director at Tokengate, a platform that allows tokenization services, for example, for real world assets (RWA) or financial instruments. Tokengate is a major player in the Zug district and the global blockchain scene[63].

On average, for cross-border transactions, there are a lot of middlemen, filters, and frictions. Technologies like blockchain make financial transactions frictionless. The potential and the tech capabilities have been built and are there.

"We have, however, the old banking and financial system, which still works and wants to keep their interests and fees intact. A financial revolution will not happen immediately," says Rieder[64].

The financial sector, by definition, is a labyrinth of regulations, and they differ at the market and nation levels. Regulation is fundamental.

> We need strong anti-money-laundering laws, and we must eradicate large-scale criminality, which thrives in new and unregulated channels. The main point, however, of the whole decentralized finance movement (DeFi) is inclusion. We need to take care of those who are unbanked today, and have no chance to participate in the global economy, as the traditional system (web2) cannot afford to let them in. All we are saying is to lower hurdles and costs, granted we need trust and safety, but we need everyone to join, which is not the case today[65].

Looking at the PYUSD case, a stable-coin could be a good bridge between the traditional and the new finance worlds. It will drive adoption of digital assets thanks to its lower volatility, especially if tied to the likes of the US dollar. But, at the same time, it has all the advantages of crypto: safety, transparency, access, interoperability with top chains and tokens, perfect for micro-transactions and programmability, making trading almost like a commodity, therefore open to whoever has an internet connection. Are PayPal and the new digital financial players going to kill established banks?

Commercial banks were born as local consultants, at the service of the community and fully trusting of their clients. They play a pivotal role in our society, which is their trust and proximity, thanks to their retail outlets. New

---

[63] For more information, see: www.tokengate.io.

[64] Rieder, Tom, Managing Director at Tokengate. Interview with Frank Pagano. 09/17/2024. Zurich.

[65] Ibid.

banks have a very compelling edge, of course, but they need to gain the trust of fans and institutions. In the end, trust remains the only "currency," so to speak, that any financial institution must achieve, protect and nurture. There is room for innovative financial platforms in the future, especially for use cases where users are willing to be in control and need no help. These services will become commodities. Things like wealth management, tax advisory, inheritance, and investments will continue to need assistance and will most likely require that human touch that we all long for while managing our assets and shaping our future.

Basic finance, which is also what the periphery of the world needs most urgently, will be outsourced to machines, with zero fees and rents. Traditional banks will adjust and focus on value-added services. New banks will need to pass the stress tests of regulators to sit at the adults' table. Technology will serve an economy that needs higher liquidity of data points and money flows. Same question as before: Are we there yet? What are the experts expecting?

By analyzing Rieder's work at Tokengate, we can say that the next few years will be critical. We are not there yet, for sure. There are, however, many signals that indicate that we could get there within the next five years. Traditional banks are experimenting with new tools. New players are getting the needed banking licenses. Markets are slowly increasing their confidence in the digital arena, and culture and literacy are improving. The future of money is a few years away from us, and it has the taste that money always had, since its invention: trust and inclusion.

Money is a tremendous enabler and liberator of resources. In a world where every bit of data and number will be tracked, we need to make sure payment rails are secure, transparent and fit for the macro and the micro. Traditional banks have a natural preference for the macro pools of profits. Technology can monetize the micro, unlocking the largest economic opportunity of human history, which is its people's lives, wants, desires and data.

Paolo Ardoino, the CEO of Tether[66], the blockchain that powers the most used stable-coin in the world (called USDT) is bullish about the potential of a decentralized currency, based on a distributed ledger. For lots of reasons. Ten years have gone by since the inception of its stable-coin, and we are only at the beginning of what its team can do for the world.

It took credit cards twenty years to be understood and used by a large portion of the public. It's unfair to judge blockchain as a failure this early, as many media outlets and financial institutions do. We have been alive for ten years, have 400 million users and 120 US $ billions of value being

---

[66] For more information, see: www.tether.to.

locked in our coins, with a strong acceleration recorded in the past three years, thanks also to the approval of new financial instruments containing crypto-currencies, like Bitcoin ETF-s for example, says Ardoino[67].

Taking the whole market of money transfers back to home countries from foreign workers, which is a key driver of growth for the receiving markets, 10% of that is done today via USDT, at a cost that is exponentially lower than the traditional money transfer avenues, dominated by entities with large rents and fees. Ardoino's venture is having an impact on the lives of those who are at the margins of the global community. The goal of Tether is, indeed, to remove all unnecessary intermediaries, helping the whole system to land in a state of simplification and augmented liquidity.

There is space for everyone, namely for a plurality of actors, in the world's financial system. The goal is not to enter a war against the banks, but to take out the filters that limit the ability of people in their ability to process payments and exchange value, while enjoying the stability of a token anchored to the US dollar. We are now looking at pegging a coin to gold, for example, or at services like tokenized financial assets, states Ardoino[68].

The potential to make the most strategic sectors of our global trade and life more efficient doesn't end here. Ardoino is working on ideas of a fair marketplace for education, where AI and the use of digital currencies for micro-transactions can stimulate training, learning, exchange across individuals and institutions, in a smart and efficient way, without middlemen who may add extra fees or barriers to a free flow of information and data, with people owning their data and their intellectual power in full thanks to individual wallets. Tether is a story of inclusion, decentralization and disintermediation, while securing the stability of stored value, which is fundamental for countries that have always suffered from geopolitical and economic volatility. People need to own their future. Ten years of hope went by. Let's hope the simplification and decentralization trends described by Ardoino continue, penetrating old and new financial actors.

4.15. The Future of Energy

One of the most critical industries of our society is energy. We need it desperately, and always at the lowest cost. Most often than not, we get it from

---

[67] Ardoino, Paolo, CEO at Tether. Interview with Frank Pagano. 10/25/2024. Lugano.
[68] Ibid.

the farthest locations, where natural elements and resources are abundant, thanks to heavy industrial equipment and complex deals with governments, on the sourcing and receiving sides of the equation. It's also an industry that must become decarbonized, while shifting geopolitical interests and equilibria. Can data help? Can Total Marketing be of support to the leaders in this field and their CEOs? Can frictionless information across supply, providers, employees, and clients help us extract and use energy at maximum efficiency, and only where and when it matters?

This is why we decided to approach Toni Volpe, who is the CEO at Nadara[69], born at the beginning of 2024 out of a merger, to create the first wind onshore provider in Europe. Owned by a private fund, and with offices in the US and Europe, it has sales of more than a billion euros and represents a leader in green energy in many European markets.

> We are a bit behind other industries in capturing, processing and using data, at least in a fully automated fashion. The merger has triggered the need, for example, of a combined data lake, where to collect and clean internal data. The priority for us is to fix the basics, when it comes to information and business relevant insights[70].

However, seamless data flows are an area of focus for the future of Nadara. From a supply chain point of view, the need for decarbonization and a lower carbon footprint has forced Nadara to move from transactional relationships with suppliers towards a collaborative and holistic approach to their inbound network. In the past, the only thing that mattered was the cost of any tender. Now, purchasing equipment needs to include cooperation and sharing of information, plans, and objectives, of course, in full respect of confidential data, but with the goal of improving the final infrastructure, thanks to the combined effort of all stakeholders.

> We need solar or wind plants that have impact and highest efficiency, so we need all hands on the deck. The metrics for success are richer than just cost *per se*. We look at how we can create a larger profit pool for all. We don't have sensors everywhere and we don't process all data automatically, but we are moving in that direction, so that every plant can turn into a live source of information. It's not as digital as it could be,

---

[69] For more information, see: www.nadara.com.

[70] Volpe, Toni, CEO at Nadara. Interview with Frank Pagano. 09/27/2024. Zurich.

but it's on my must-do list. Plus, we need to do this at scale, for better and better future energy factories[71].

The same principle applies to employees and partners, humans so to speak, who work in corporate roles or maintenance. Besides health and safety, which is key, tracking and monitoring people will allow the company to move from schedule-based interventions to proactive and predictive actions, based on the actual conditions of the equipment, thus reducing costs and capturing real life data, which again can be leveraged for innovation, consistency of supply, and higher value-added services towards our final customers. The relationship with larger, direct key accounts, for example, moves into the same open and collaborative direction. Today, it's done more via a manual exchange, but it will move into a fully automated flow, with immediate actions taken by machines, which will ensure consistency and optimization of all services.

Exponential technologies, like AI, are being used for maintenance and, slowly but progressively, also for advisory tasks; for example, those linked to the analysis of energy consumption numbers. The human contribution is still present, and it can be replaced by machines in the medium term, thus generating efficiencies and, again, new profit pools. According to Volpe[72], efficiencies in the whole industry may be at least around 15%, and it could be more in a scenario of seamless and instant data flows and actions triggered by artificial intelligence. If we draw the line, future energy will be green, and it will remain a commodity, with an increasingly lower cost, especially thanks to tech advancements. Companies like Nadara will have to complement their sales with higher value-added services. It's a long road. But it's happening. This is why Volpe is internalizing world-class human and artificial intelligence.

Total Marketing and regulations will bring the world to a future where energy will be 100% from green sources, while being compelling from a pricing point of view. We'll direct energy, and the manpower associated with it, where it matters, when it's needed, while sweating our assets in an intelligent way. The capillary equipment, distributed globally and physically on the earth's surface, could capture more data than just what's needed to manufacture megawatts, turning energy mills into data factories for land, sea, sky, and livestock, just to name a few, and exploding the economic value associated with their operations. Volpe is used to change, and so are Nadara and its owners. The industry will need machines to run the future green watts' show like a clock, and humans to add more green to the green.

---

[71] Ibid.

[72] Ibid.

4.16. The Future of Banking

To understand the impact of technology on our society at large, we should visit geographies that are perceived as tangential to the heart of the global economy. As a matter of fact, very often the best innovations pop up far away from the big financial capitals. This is why we talk to Rob Downes, Head of Digital Delivery and Digital Assets at Absa Corporate and Investment Bank, one of the most important banks in South Africa and on the whole continent[73]. Downes is a "Brit," who dedicated the last 20 years of his life to banking on the African scene, and he is experimenting with high-tech solutions to evolve the role and scope of traditional banks. What's the future of banks, especially in those contexts where resources are limited, transactions are measurable, and banks can make the difference in supporting the growth of families, communities and companies?

Would you like to send some money abroad in Africa? You might hire a taxi driver, hand them the equivalent of $100, and see $80 delivered. Western Union from Dubai to India, known as the classic emigrants' remit to their families, would see a similar trimming. Can tech help us do better, without breaking the bank itself, which has overhead and other fixed costs to maintain?

We are experimenting with AI and blockchain, on custody, exchange, stable-coins, and especially cross-border payments, as you can imagine. We offer clients the trust of a regulated institution, and we guarantee customer protection and security, while processing transactions at lower fees, which is good for the bank and private individuals and companies[74].

Absa has been experimenting and innovating with alternative assets based on blockchain technologies. The tests and experiments are fundamental to explore new areas, and potentially new streams of revenue for the bank.

The number one priority is to understand where machines can do a better job at serving clients at best, while protecting their privacy and safety. Efficiencies can be gained, for example, in the whole merchants' fees segment, now dominated by credit card operators, in trade finance and invoicing processing across countries, which may entail multiple layers of currencies and local banks.

Decentralized ledgers and programmable money are probably the best way to dramatically reduce filters and fees, in full security for all stakeholders. We are embarking into proofs-of-concepts, which - given the delicate context of finance - will take years to finesse and scale,

---

[73] For more information, see: www.absa.africa.

[74] Downes, Rob, Head of Digital Delivery and Digital Assets at Absa Corporate and Investment Bank. Interview with Frank Pagano. 10/02/2024. Zug.

which is natural in our industry. We need to comply with all regulations. Our reputation and branding are our most important asset, and the number one reason customers pick a bank like ours for their finances[75].

New profit pools, thanks to exponential technologies, come from programs like custody of crypto assets or wealth management initiatives involving crypto as an alternative investment. Approximately six million South Africans hold some cryptocurrencies today, so Absa needs to have a product offering that may recruit these crypto natives, while neutralizing risks for the bank's books, who are attending summits and meetings of the tech communities in Switzerland, on top of the traditional financial gatherings. It makes sense: Finance will become more and more FinTech, as the cool kids of these days and hip venture capitalists repeat *ad nauseam*.

The financial market is strictly regulated by national and international rules. Digital currencies are still in stealth mode: the digital Yuan, from China, did not take off; the Nigerian CBDC is still very small; the digital Euro is in the making; stable-coins are measurable, and investors tend to concentrate on the largest opportunity out there, which is Bitcoin. Looking at digital and pure bank plays, like Revolut or N26, these firms are still national, if not Regional.

Downes is getting ready for a new world, which will be exponentially more digital than today. His team and his bank need to adopt new tech tools and adapt the culture of traditional banks at the same time. To do that, any organization needs a strong push from the top, and from the CEO. The test phase is usually a no-brainer, but it's the scale-up part where the C-Room needs to align, hold hands and set the pace for change. The execution is usually a matter of small and focused cross-functional teams, executing against a roadmap blessed from the top and communicated widely to the whole hierarchy of the bank, like in the case of Absa.

Let's look at the other side of the banking world. What's a crypto bank? Is there such a thing? How do they work, compared to traditional banking institutions? Amina Bank[76], formerly known as Seba and with offices across the globe, wants to be the bank of choice for crypto innovators and trailblazers, and start-ups or scale-ups operating in the so-called Web 3 space.

To know more about this world, we speak to Myles Harrison, Amina's Chief Product Officer. The crypto community wants and needs access to traditional banking services, like for example a simple checking account, to process payments, or needs help to hold their assets. For the moment, Amina serves

---

[75] Ibid.

[76] For more information, see: www.aminagroup.com.

especially the portion of the Web 3 space that has accumulated wealth via cryptocurrencies and blockchain-related programs, so high-net-worth individuals, who need support with their crypto-assets from a different kind of wealth manager. This is in line with the mandate and regulations of authorities like Finma[77] (Switzerland). In this respect, they function as a traditional bank for a new group of asset holders, which may not find a home elsewhere. On the B2B, or corporate, side, they are also best placed to cater to those Web3 start-uPs that may not find a way to do their banking via the traditional network. This is the most recent add to Amina's portfolio.

Serving the right start-uPs, who have a vision and a plan to change the world, may be a shortcut to help the world evolve towards higher inclusion and liquidity.

> Start-uPs are a force of financial change, and we want to be their bank, exactly like in the old days, banks were at the service of entrepreneurs and merchants, who wanted to create value for themselves and their communities. This is a part of our product roadmap and essential to our vision. There is more. We also have a B2B2C product offering, designed for non-crypto and traditional banks, like Julius Baer for example, who use our infrastructure and products to provide crypto services to their client base. Julius Baer's services span from custody to trading, to staking. This is a quick way to boost penetration of new tools across traditional audiences[78].

Retail banking will most likely become a commodity in a world run by AI and blockchain. Financial competition will move towards high-value-added services, like wealth management and custody, besides familiarity with alternative types of securities. Amina wants to become the go-to solution provider for new tribes and products. For example, products like crypto currencies' collateralized lending are something that they offer, in a safe and secure way, for everyone. Today, they handle over twenty coins, with strict scrutiny on the demand and supply side, in line with regulations. The bank must innovate and fully comply at the same time.

Stable-coins are another area of growth, where Amina intends to be on the leaders' camp, from PYUSD (PayPal's stable-coin) to USDC.[79]

---

[77] Finma is the Swiss federal supervisory authority for financial markets. For more information, see: www.finma.ch.

[78] Harrison, Myles, Chief Product Officer at Amina Bank. Interview with Frank Pagano. 11/06/2024. Zurich.

[79] Amina offers two stable-coins from Circle: USDC (Circle) and EURC. Circle is a blockchain powered financial and payment platform.

Transparency and trust are key ingredients of any bank. Amina embraces those, for example, with features like proof of reserves or proof of key for wallets, fully respecting privacy, but with the goal of reassuring clients around its backing solidity and zero tolerance of shortcuts and tricks. Amina is a case of a new financial actor, who becomes the partner of new communities and the sidekick of traditional financial actors in their evolution towards enhanced digitization and innovation. It's not a war against the old world. It doesn't need to be a zero-sum game.

The future of banking tastes like the past, namely trust, privacy and safety. The future of traditional banks also needs to have a futuristic after-taste, made of zero unnecessary fees and costs, especially on payments and money transfers, and high value-added consulting on wealth management and investment opportunities, from credit to mortgages, to collaterals hedged against new digital assets, to deep expertise on the new families of digital currencies coming up, regionally and globally. This will need a workforce that is tech-savvy, without the greedy deviations that the crypto brothers or the Wall Street wolves showed as their number one priority.

AI will change the face of our most strategic industries, from energy to education, to banking and finance. We will need all hands on deck and some guidance, in terms of regional rules, especially on the treatment of personal data. Total Marketing will become the norm, which means that companies will be interested in marketing their existence to and trading with suppliers, employees, and fans. How does that transformation occur? How can a CEO make this happen within legacy systems and established cultures across their company? What happens to the way a firm operates?

Bibliography

Generative AI could raise global GDP by 7%, Goldman Sachs, April 2023.

Gilbert, Daniel. *Stumbling on Happiness*, Vintage, 2007.

Global Risks Report 2024, The World Economic Forum, January 2024.

Kahneman Daniel, Olivier Sibony and Cass R. Sunstein. *Noise: A Flaw in Human Judgment*, Little, Brown Spark, 2021.

Lawrence, Jerome and Robert E. Lee. *Inherit the Wind: The Powerful Drama of the Greatest Courtroom Clash of the Century*, Ballantine Books, 2003.

Reimagining Digital ID, The World Economic Forum, June 2023.

Schwab, Klaus and Peter Vanham. *Stakeholder Capitalism: A Global Economy that Works for Progress, People and Planet*, Wiley, 2021.

Shaping the Future of Learning: The Role of AI in Education 4.0, The World Economic Forum, April 2024.

Your employer is (probably) unprepared for artificial intelligence, *The Economist*, July 16th, 2023.

Chapter Five
Diary of a Transformation Madman

Cecilia Marchi[1]
Marco Di Dio Roccazzella
Frank Pagano

5.1 Reality Shows

It is happening in real life. The Total Marketing, or TM, model is a transformative framework that offers a holistic approach towards stronger and more integrated relationships across the value chain. For example, in industries like Fast-Moving Consumer Goods (FMCG) and Fashion, where customer loyalty, operational efficiency, and brand perception are critical, TM can drive significant improvements by aligning customer, employee, supplier, and overall brand experiences into one cohesive strategy. The following are illustrative applications in these two industries. We steal with pride from our experience in the business "jungle," showcasing how TM principles can enhance market performance.

In FMCG, the focus on supplier experience is vital. We[2] have built several digital platforms to enable real-time collaboration with suppliers, for example, providing access to accurate demand forecasts, which help suppliers plan production and inventory more effectively. Moreover, sustainability initiatives are integrated into supplier relationships, encouraging the sourcing of eco-friendly materials and reducing environmental impact. This alignment positions the brand as a responsible partner, fostering stronger partnerships and improving quality consistency. TM helps to ensure that suppliers are seen as critical stakeholders in the business, expanding the potential and value of the overall supply chain.

On the employees' front, FMCG companies empower their workforce through the adoption of advanced digital tools and comprehensive training programs. Frontline workers, particularly in manufacturing and logistics, are equipped with real-time monitoring systems and predictive maintenance tools

---

[1] Associate Partner, Jakala.

[2] The 'we' refers to the output of consultancies like Jakala, where the three authors of this chapter belong. This is true for most MarTech agencies and companies.

that improve operational efficiency and reduce downtime. Companies invest heavily in the continuous development of their employees, offering opportunities to advance their skills in various areas, from operations to customer relations. This approach ensures that employees feel more engaged and capable, which not only boosts productivity but also innovation. By focusing on people empowerment, TM helps to create a more motivated and capable workforce, driving operational excellence, and higher customer satisfaction.

When it comes to the Customer Experience, FMCG brands usually utilize data analytics and artificial intelligence to deeply understand consumer preferences and behaviors. Personalized marketing campaigns target specific segments of the market, offering tailored promotions based on individual needs and preferences. Moreover, an omnichannel approach ensures that customers experience a seamless journey, whether they are shopping online, in-store, or through other channels. Integrated CRM systems (Customer Relationship Management) track customer interactions, enabling companies to deliver personalized services, which foster loyalty and increase customer lifetime value. TM's integration of technology and data-driven insights into customer engagement helps to create a more meaningful and personalized relationship with fans, making them feel valued and understood.

FMCG firms are increasingly leveraging neuromarketing to gain deeper insights into consumer behavior and product interactions. This happens in the phase of product tests, before the in-market launch. By using techniques such as eye-tracking, brain wave analysis (via electroencephalography, or EEG), and facial coding, they can study how consumers react to different packaging designs, product placements, and pricing strategies. These neuro-based insights allow companies to understand unconscious preferences and emotional responses, which are often not revealed through traditional market research. As a result, businesses can optimize packaging, branding, and pricing decisions to better align with consumer desires, ultimately driving more effective marketing strategies and increasing sales. Sometimes, they also analyze consumer behavior in real-life settings by utilizing consumer panels, which track in-home product usage. Through this method, panel participants provide detailed insights into how products are used, how often they are consumed, and what factors influence their purchasing decisions. Companies combine this data with technologies like smart sensors or mobile apps that monitor and record daily usage patterns. By observing these behaviors in a natural environment, FMCG brands can better understand how their products fit into consumers' routines, identify pain points or unmet needs, and refine their offerings to enhance satisfaction and loyalty.

Lastly, brand experience in FMCG is increasingly shaped by commitments to sustainability and transparency. Brands emphasize ethical practices, such as reducing plastic waste and carbon emissions, while also providing clear and transparent product information regarding sourcing, production, and environmental impact. These initiatives resonate strongly with eco-conscious consumers, further reinforcing the brand's identity as a leader in sustainability. TM enables brands to align their messaging with these values, building trust not only with customers but also with employees and suppliers who share these commitments.

The fashion industry also reaps significant benefits from applying a TM model, particularly on the supply side. Fashion brands often collaborate closely with their suppliers to meet ambitious sustainability goals, using innovative materials like recycled polyester and organic cotton. Transparency is a key component of these partnerships, with some brands employing blockchain technology to track the origin of materials, ensuring that suppliers and customers alike can verify ethical sourcing practices. This approach strengthens the bond between brands and suppliers, fostering a culture of innovation and sustainability. TM's role in enhancing supplier relationships in fashion promotes not only operational efficiency but also strengthens the brand's environmental credentials.

In terms of employees' experience, fashion companies empower their design and retail teams through cutting-edge technology. Design teams are provided with tools like 3D printing and digital rendering software, which enable faster prototyping and reduce the time to market for new products. Meanwhile, retail employees are equipped with mobile devices that give them real-time access to customer data and inventory information, allowing them to offer personalized service and make informed recommendations, on the spot and in an almost predictive way. This level of employee empowerment leads to increased creativity in product development and more personalized interactions with customers, driving satisfaction and loyalty. TM's emphasis on employee engagement ensures that teams are better equipped to innovate and deliver an exceptional service.

Customer experience in fashion is increasingly driven by personalized, omnichannel engagement. Fashion brands leverage customer data to offer bespoke services, such as custom product design or tailored workout recommendations, via membership programs. These programs build emotional connections with consumers, thanks to exclusive offers and personalized content. Additionally, brands create digital ecosystems through their mobile apps, where customers can shop, track fitness goals, or access exclusive content, seamlessly integrating retail with other aspects of their lifestyle. TM's approach to customer engagement in fashion leverages personalization to create stronger emotional bonds with consumers, increasing their lifetime value.

In the context of the TM framework, clienteling apps, with excellent user experience, and used by sales associates in luxury boutiques, can significantly enhance both Customer Experience and Employee Experience. When these apps are augmented by AI-powered chatbots, which analyze CRM data and customer preferences, sales associates are empowered with real-time and personalized insights. This allows them to offer more tailored recommendations and seamless interactions, leading to higher customer satisfaction. At the same time, the streamlined process reduces the cognitive load on employees, improving their overall experience and productivity, and accelerates the achievement of their sales targets.

CRM data and consumer purchasing patterns play a crucial role in enhancing merchandising strategies. Brands can gain valuable insights into consumer preferences, buying habits, and seasonal trends. This information enables merchandisers to define more effective collection grids, which align closely with demand. For instance, understanding which styles, colors, and sizes are popular among specific customer segments allows brands to curate their collections, minimizing excess inventory (and waste) and maximizing sales potential. Additionally, integrating CRM insights with real-time sales data helps brands anticipate shifts in consumer behavior, enabling them to adapt their merchandising strategies proactively. Ultimately, leveraging CRM data fosters a more responsive and customer-centric approach to merchandising, ensuring that collections resonate with consumers and drive profitability.

In retail, the use of in-store cameras in boutiques provides valuable insights into customer behavior and interactions within the store environment, all of it while respecting GDPR, of course. By monitoring how customers navigate the space, which displays capture their attention, and where they tend to linger, retailers can gather crucial data on product desirability and store layout effectiveness. These insights enable brands to optimize product placement, enhancing visual merchandising strategies that align with customer preferences. Furthermore, understanding the customer flow inside a store secures effective staff scheduling, protecting peak times and high-traffic areas.

Finally, brand experiences in fashion are closely tied to social responsibility and sustainability. Brands champion various causes, such as environmental conservation, racial equality, and gender empowerment, aligning their messaging with the values of their core audience. Sustainability initiatives, from carbon emissions reduction to circular designs, become central to the brand's identity, attracting customers and employees who prioritize ethical practices. TM facilitates the integration of purpose-driven messaging into brand strategy, helping fashion companies connect with consumers and employees on a deeper and values-driven level.

FMCG and fashion are two industries that are very well versed with data processing and insights. They have already built bridges and interfaces for a healthy dialogue across suppliers, employees and users. Total Marketing is just distorting their capabilities and the potential of personalized and predictive experiences across channels. How can any industry get there?

5.2. How Can You Do It?

One of the core principles of the TM model is the recognition that all stakeholders are interdependent. Optimizing the experience of one group has a positive impact on the others. For example, improving employee satisfaction can lead to better customer service, while stronger supplier relationships enhance product quality and perfect delivery.

The TM model needs, first, shared platforms for collaboration, where customers, employees, and suppliers can interact in real time. This fosters better communication, reduces friction, and encourages innovation across the entire value chain. Real-time data sharing is essential, allowing stakeholders to make informed decisions based on up-to-date insights. Therefore, the first question is: do we have the right tools and platforms across all stakeholders? Plus, can we fix the basics, namely, what data are we capturing and why?

Transparency and trust are fundamental to fostering strong relationships along the entire value chain. By ensuring that all business practices are ethical and transparent, companies can build trust with their suppliers, employees, and customers, enhancing the overall experience for all parties involved. On the other side, the right tech stack can help to obfuscate confidential details while aggregating relevant facts, which are vital for a smooth flow of business-critical insights from suppliers to fans, and vice versa.

So, it's technology and an attitude of trust and transparency, which will trigger a culture of change. The TM model celebrates a value chain that is interconnected, making it an ecosystem where each component – design, manufacturing, distribution, sales, and post-sales – must work harmoniously to maximize value for everyone. Let's look at each step, one by one. This will provide a checklist for managers out there, and it will make us understand why pooling data can change the life of any company.

5.2.1. Design

The collaboration between brand, suppliers, and employees is critical in designing products that meet market demand while adhering to sustainability and ethical standards. In the upstream stage, the supplier and employee experiences play a significant role in shaping how a product is developed and conceptualized. Suppliers provide essential materials and components, while employees contribute creativity, technical skills, and innovation.

TM in the design phase, in detail:

- Cross-team collaboration: Digital platforms, powered by AI and cloud-based tools, can facilitate real-time interaction among designers, engineers, and suppliers. This allows for co-creation. Such collaboration reduces the time-to-market and ensures that products are aligned with both brand vision and market trends.

- Ethical and sustainable sourcing: In today's environmentally conscious marketplace, it's crucial to ensure that materials are sourced ethically. Brands must work with suppliers, ensuring that raw materials are not only high-quality but also ethically produced. Transparency in sourcing enhances the brand's reputation and attracts eco-conscious customers, while employees feel proud to work for a company that prioritizes social responsibility. The use of technologies like blockchain to record transactions and specs protects the fan from malicious actors or shortcuts, and reduces time to verdict in case of conflict and controversies, minimizing legal expenses on all fronts.

- Feedback integration: Early feedback from suppliers and employees on design feasibility, cost-efficiency, and innovation potential allows for better decision-making. By involving stakeholders at this stage, the entire value chain becomes more adaptive, efficient, and collaborative. Digital prototyping, 3D rendering, and simulation software solutions are some examples, explored in the previous chapters, which make design better informed and more likely to meet the brief of design leads.

In this phase, supplier collaboration platforms that facilitate real-time interaction play a pivotal role. Brand teams and suppliers communicate effortlessly to align on product expectations, which minimizes errors and maximizes efficiency.

5.2.2. Manufacturing

Manufacturing represents a critical nexus, where suppliers continue to influence the value chain, while company teams become key. The relationship between suppliers and employees during production determines not only product quality but also operational efficiency.

Here is TM in manufacturing, in detail:

- Automation and AI-driven processes: Manufacturing is heavily dependent on process optimization, and modern AI-based technologies enhance productivity and accuracy. Predictive analytics and automation reduce human error, ensuring that products are made to exact specifications and deadlines. This also enhances the Employee Experience by reducing repetitive manual tasks and allowing them to focus on more meaningful and creative work.

- Supplier reliability: Thanks to tech touchpoints, powered again by AI, suppliers deliver materials and components on time, in full and where needed. Through advanced data-sharing systems and real-time communication, any potential disruptions (such as delays or quality issues) can be addressed proactively. This integration allows manufacturers to adjust schedules and inventory management in ways that minimize production downtime and maintain product quality, zeroing stock ruptures and missed orders.

- Quality assurance: Close collaboration between suppliers and employees ensures that quality control measures are in place, which is crucial for maintaining brand integrity. Employees benefit from having the tools and training to oversee quality, while suppliers are incentivized to deliver consistently high-quality materials.

Through seamless integration of supplier and employee interfaces, manufacturing enjoys maximum efficiency and productivity while upholding the standards set by the brand.

5.2.3. Distribution

As products move downstream in the value chain, toward distribution and sales, the Customer Experience becomes the dominant focus. However, supplier and brand experiences remain critical, as they ensure that products are delivered to customers efficiently and consistently.

Here is TM in distribution, in detail:

- Logistics and real-time tracking: Leveraging advanced logistics platforms, businesses track product shipments in real time, providing customers with up-to-date information on delivery status. This transparency builds trust and enhances Customer Experience. Suppliers, in turn, can manage their resources better by aligning with real-time demand, thus reducing bottlenecks and delays.

- Seamless omnichannel fulfillment: Whether a customer purchases a product online or in a physical store, the brand must ensure that the experience is consistent. A robust omnichannel strategy ensures that products are readily available through multiple channels, including direct-to-consumer websites, third-party marketplaces, or retail stores. The tech integration across all channels creates a seamless and unified interaction for customers, whether they are shopping online, engaging with customer service, or visiting a store.

- Supplier coordination: Distribution relies on close coordination with logistics partners and suppliers to ensure timely delivery. Miscommunication or inefficiencies at this stage can negatively impact Customer Experience and brand reputation. Integrated digital platforms unlock real-time updates, better forecasting and effective coordination, which benefit both suppliers and customers.

This phase highlights the need for streamlined logistics, optimized supply chain management, and robust communication across all stakeholders. The final result is a seamless Customer Experience, where expectations for timely delivery and product availability are always met.

5.2.4. Sales and Post-Sales

Sales and post-sales support are critical to driving customer loyalty and long-term brand success. While the Customer Experience is at the forefront here, the interactions between employees, customers and the brand remain integral to success and perfect execution.

Here is TM in sales and post-sales, in detail:

- Personalized selling and AI-driven insights: The use of AI-driven analytics allows brands to offer personalized product recommendations. Employees use these insights to better serve customers while enhancing their own productivity and job satisfaction. When customers receive personalized offers that cater to their needs, this improves both the sales experience and the perception of the brand.

- Post-purchase support and customer engagement: Customer experiences continue through support services, whether it's assistance with product installation, troubleshooting, or returns. Brands that offer proactive support, such as predictive maintenance alerts or seamless return processes, build deeper relationships with customers. Employees handling customer service must be equipped with the right tools, such as AI-driven chatbots and CRM systems, to ensure fast and accurate responses.

- Customer feedback and iteration: Continuous feedback loops from customers should inform future product development, marketing strategies, and employee training. By collecting and acting on this feedback, brands can ensure that they are always improving their service, which in turn improves employee satisfaction, as they see their efforts contributing to a positive business performance.

This phase emphasizes the importance of post-sales interactions, where employees must be empowered to provide excellent customer service, and customers must feel that their needs are being met long after the purchase. Customer service has always been considered a tier two touchpoint. The Total Marketing model reinterprets each interface as primary media. There is no data point that is secondary and ancillary. All facts and experiences, big or small, contribute to excellent service across the whole value chain.

5.3. So Far, So Good. Questions Anyone?

Unlike traditional models, which often focus on isolated areas of engagement, the TM model integrates every interaction within the business ecosystem into one cohesive strategy. This integration drives engagement, loyalty, and trust across the board by tying together the experiences of customers, employees, suppliers, and the brand itself. However, some considerations must be raised when implementing such a comprehensive model. The growing importance of data in enabling this interconnectedness presents both opportunities and challenges. Additionally, the role of artificial intelligence (AI) as a key driver of TM's personalization and automation demands deeper exploration.

Furthermore, implementing the TM model involves complexities not only from a technological standpoint but also from an organizational and cultural perspective. Whether this model is more suited to small, medium, or large enterprises is an important question, as each faces unique hurdles in adopting it. The ethical implications of data sharing, privacy concerns, and the potential need to reward stakeholders who contribute their information also emerge as critical issues. The opportunity here is that the TM model can reduce information asymmetry, which could lead to positive externalities and even a fundamental shift in business models. The following sections delve into these considerations, offering a deeper understanding of both the benefits and the risks inherent in adopting the TM framework.

5.3.1. The Role of Tech and Humans

At the heart of the TM model lies the importance of data. Data sharing across all stakeholders—customers, employees, suppliers, or brands—is critical to the success of the TM approach. Information drives decision-making, optimizes interactions, and enhances the ability to personalize experiences across the value chain. In an age where digital interactions are increasingly the norm, businesses must be equipped to collect, analyze, and act on vast amounts of data.

Data-sharing platforms enable real-time communication between suppliers and internal teams, enhancing collaboration and ensuring that customer preferences, supply chain demands, and employee inputs are aligned. Sharing data reduces information asymmetry, where one party knows more than another, leading to smoother operations, more accurate forecasts, and higher trust between stakeholders.

The reduction of information asymmetry through enhanced data sharing can generate positive externalities for the entire business ecosystem. By creating transparency in the flow of information, businesses can foster stronger relationships with their suppliers, customers, and employees, while also paving the way for innovation. This could even lead to a revolution in traditional business models, where open and collaborative ecosystems thrive on shared insights and collaborative value creation[3]. A shared ecosystem holds all actors accountable and keeps them honest, given the transparency of each interaction and transaction.

Implementing the TM model is not without its challenges. From a technological perspective, integrating AI, data analytics, and real-time communication platforms requires substantial investment, especially for companies with legacy systems. The integration of various data points across different stakeholder experiences demands a robust technological infrastructure capable of supporting real-time data collection, processing, and sharing.

Organizationally, the adoption of TM also involves a cultural shift. Companies must break down internal silos, fostering collaboration between traditionally separate departments like marketing, sales, HR, and supply chain management. Employees need to be trained to use new technologies and understand the broader implications of their roles within a more interconnected value chain.

Many organizations struggle to find individuals with the diverse skill sets required to effectively execute Total Marketing initiatives, including data analysis, digital marketing, customer relationship management, and cross-channel integration. These skill gaps often result in fragmented marketing

---

[3] There could be some similarities with the Servant Leadership model, which dates back to the 1970's. The model is centered around service to the stakeholders' and subordinates' interests, rather than the leaders' ones. There is, indeed, a stress to the open flow of data, which may create a broader pool of value for all, instead of catering to the leading group first. Our contention here is slightly different: free flow of data, and a smart way of refining data into actionable insights for all, will make our companies, communities and all stakeholders better off. We don't divide the world into servants and leaders. The TM model looks at consumers, employees, suppliers and shareholders as peers, and contributors, into an open network of data generation, capture and crunching. The data ownership is probably more strategic than the individuals leading each pole or group, inside the multi-modal network designed by Gartner. If anything, data will make that 'servant' leadership sharper, closer to reality, more efficient and effective. Again, our goal is to elevate marketing models, rather than replace them.

efforts that fail to deliver a cohesive brand message, ultimately undermining customer engagement and loyalty. Furthermore, the rapid evolution of marketing technologies demands continuous learning and adaptation, making it difficult for existing teams to keep pace. As a result, businesses may miss out on the full potential of Total Marketing, limiting their ability to foster meaningful connections with customers and enhance overall marketing effectiveness. Addressing this talent shortage is crucial for organizations seeking to thrive in an increasingly competitive landscape.

For many organizations, this transition can be daunting, particularly for larger companies with complex hierarchies and established ways of working. This leads to the question: Is the TM model easier to implement in small, medium, or large companies? While smaller organizations may be more agile and able to adopt these new systems more quickly, they often lack the financial and technological resources required for large-scale data integration and AI-driven systems. On the other hand, larger companies may have the capital to invest in the necessary infrastructure but may struggle with the organizational inertia that often accompanies change. Medium-sized companies may find themselves in a sweet spot, with both the agility and the resources to make the transition smoother, though they will still face their own unique challenges.

A key consideration in the TM model is how data is shared between stakeholders and whether there are incentives for doing so. In a system where customers and suppliers share valuable data with brands, be it purchasing behavior, preferences, or operational metrics, there is a growing argument that these stakeholders should be rewarded. Suppliers could benefit from enhanced collaboration and visibility into demand forecasts, while customers might expect personalized discounts, loyalty rewards, or even more intuitive, tailored product offerings. This is exactly what we saw in our preceding chapters: giving data some value will create new profit pools and stimulate all stakeholders to comply and execute to perfection. On the other side, failure to join a data sharing ecosystem or comply may facilitate conflict resolution cases and help brands identify malicious actors along the food chain.

However, the sharing of data also raises important concerns around privacy and security. As data flows between customers, suppliers, employees, and brands, the risk of data breaches and misuse increases. Companies must invest heavily in data security infrastructure to ensure that sensitive information is protected from cyber threats. This not only safeguards the interests of the business but also maintains the trust of all stakeholders.

The issue of data privacy also touches on ethical considerations. Businesses must navigate the fine line between leveraging data to enhance experiences and respecting the privacy of all stakeholders. With increasing regulations, like GDPR and other data protection laws, brands need to be transparent about how data is collected, stored, and used, ensuring that stakeholders are informed and consenting.

5.3.2. Ethical Implications

Ethics play a crucial role in the TM model, particularly as businesses seek to create a more interconnected and transparent value chain.

On one hand, ethical concerns relate to data privacy and the responsible use of AI. Brands must ensure that AI algorithms are fair, unbiased, and transparent, especially when they influence decisions that affect employees, customers, or suppliers. On the other hand, the ethical treatment of suppliers and employees is central to the TM framework. Businesses are increasingly held accountable for their supply chain practices, particularly in terms of sustainability and labor rights. As brands strive for greater transparency and collaboration with suppliers, they must also ensure that their partners adhere to ethical standards, including fair wages, safe working conditions, and environmental sustainability. In this sense, the TM model is not just about creating better business outcomes, but also about fostering a fairer and more equitable ecosystem.

In conclusion, the TM model represents a significant evolution in how businesses interact with all stakeholders, but it also brings with it a host of considerations and concerns. Data and AI are essential, enabling businesses to deliver personalized and consistent experiences across the value chain. However, the complexity of a ™ approach, from both technological and organizational perspectives, requires careful planning, investment, and cultural adaptation.

Data sharing lies at the heart of TM, offering the potential for reducing information asymmetry and transforming business models. Stakeholders must be properly incentivized to share their data, and businesses must address the critical issues of privacy and security to maintain trust. Ethical considerations, from responsible AI use to fair supplier practices, must be integrated into the framework to ensure that it not only enhances business performance but also contributes to a more responsible and sustainable future.

The journey to adopting the TM model is neither simple nor immediate, but for businesses willing to embrace this new paradigm, the final reward — increased loyalty, efficiency, and brand value — can be transformative.

5.4. Conclusions

The TM framework offers a sustainable path to move beyond the traditional focus on individualism and competition. Total Marketing is all about a new paradigm, which merges individualism and competition with an outlook into the broader community and network of players around a company. Success is no longer the result of programs just centered on the brand fan, who continues to be the ultimate focus of any business, but rather of the collective work and contribution of the entire community of employees, customers, and partners.

To ensure the sustainability of the planet, we must reshape the world around data, rather than molding data to fit outdated systems. This highlights the necessity of a collective effort for a sustainable future. A data-driven approach enables more accurate insights for enhanced business and environmental impact, steering individuals and organizations toward more sustainable practices and an overall larger business opportunity for all. The adoption of this approach can orient behaviors in the right direction and expose actors within the system who fraudulently or dominantly capture value. However, this requires a complete redesign of processes, organizational structures, and potentially the entire economic system. Despite these challenges, it opens the door to more inclusive, ethical, and sustainable growth for companies and society. It all starts with the right questions around tech and humans, or, as we say in business jargon, company culture.

The big difference in the age of exponential technologies is that AI and blockchain, for example, can help us shape the business of the future and transform our culture and networks at the same time. The big difference is that we could get the data and insights to change. The difference is that now we know. The next step would be to own the change process. Right, who owns it?

Conclusions, Own It

Mara Cassinari
Frank Pagano

If you want change, for real, you should own it. What change do we want, though? There are four big battles that the world needs to win: technological breakthroughs, sustainability, collaborative marketing (in the broader sense of the term: engagement, dialogue), and a mindset of change.

There is a common thread across the four items, which is the power of the 'us' before the 'I'. Being able to dominate and make sense of the communal data that we produce will be key if we want to act for a smarter, safer, cooperative, and open-minded world. If you will, sustainability[1], as we said earlier, should be remarketed under the umbrella of a Total Marketing approach to our businesses and communities. Efficiencies can be realized faster, thanks to a wide penetration and clever use of exponential technologies.

This is why the adoption of a mindset of change is probably the priority item for any organization or company. The theory of a talking product and of a talking consumer is a few years from materializing, so the most important and urgent shift that we need to work on is our culture, processes, and people.

Now, looking at corporations, or at startups and scaleups as a matter of fact, who owns change?

As a gut reaction, it should be a mythical figure that combines the skills of Chief Technology Officer, Chief Information Officer, Chief Human Resources Officer, Chief Marketing Officer, Chief Experience Officer, and CEO. Like a unicorn, this hero can master tech, people, communication and leadership abilities, all at once, with a pinch of futuristic vision as to where the world is going. The short answer is: This is not going to happen. We need speed and scale in a digital transformation, and technology will help us for sure. But we need a structural adjustment to our organizational chart, so that change can flow faster and deeper through the corporate layers or through any organization. We need ownership.

---

[1] If we take the acronym ESG, at least in its E component (Environment), data pooling, free flow and exchange leads to exponentially better efficiencies in resources' allocation and utilization.

We would suggest at this point three scenarios, which could be of help for a reader who wants to move into action mode. The recommendation is to craft the right organizational set-up, so that roles and responsibilities are in place, budgets have been disbursed, objectives clarified, and all that's needed is, in the end, just a perfect execution of a shared master plan.

Here are our three scenarios:

- The creation, inside the C-Room, of a new role, called Chief Transformation Officer, whose mandate is to evolve the organization towards set objectives (KPIs), to maintain the tempo of the change and to constantly report back to the CEO and the Board. The Key Performance Indicators (KPI) should be wrapped around the four battles that we mentioned: adoption of what exponential technology and when; road to a fully sustainable company, in line with international treaties (Net Zero by 2030); creation of the infrastructure that allows all departments to have fast and fluid exchange with all stakeholders, internal and external; continuous training for reskilling and upskilling, to design a future proof organization. There are plenty of examples of this first scenario. Often, the Chief Strategy Officer enlarges their title and scope of action to include transformation as a priority at a global level.

- The birth of a small committee of Chiefs, inside the C-Room, coordinated by the CEO, who takes full responsibility for the digital and cultural transformation of its organization. Same KPIs as above, but with a clear and direct, almost personal engagement of the CEO in the workings of the organization of the future. There are plenty of CEOs who are directly involved in how their companies jump into new horizons, especially in mid-sized enterprises. This could be the case for large corporations, too, like for the transformation path headed by Björn Rosengren, CEO at ABB between 2020-2024.

- The merge of the roles of the Chief Marketing Officer and Chief Information & Technology Officer. Marketing has always been the 'eye' of the consumer inside a company. Marketing has always entailed data collection and insight generation to maximize the impact of offering any company proposition to the market. The superpowers provided by technology should allow a marketer to leverage well-oiled skills for the construction of the highways of mutual communication with communities, suppliers, agencies, employees and users. The KPIs would be the same as those listed above for the other two scenarios. The big change is that the integration of the loop of suppliers, employees and consumers will feed new life into the organization, with trickle-down effects on product innovation, advertising, trade and investors' relationships, customer care, and so forth, giving new life to marketing and business acumen to tech stack procurement. One example of this third scenario is Coop Switzerland, where the CIO/CTO and CMO were merged into one role some ten years ago. Coop is a retailer, trading other people's stuff into buyers' shopping carts. This specific example seems extremely interesting as to how tech can make that match between brands and fans seamless on a physical and digital turf. Can this scenario also happen for a non-retailer?

One thing is sure. The leader of the future will need to be more technologically savvy vs. the previous generations, boomers and Gen X-ers especially. Tech literacy needs to be accompanied and preceded by love for data, and for people above all, with the clear idea of building a long-term roadmap, to make any company a tech-driven, sustainable, communicative and open to its broader community. The first and the second scenarios have one major risk: the temptation to focus on numbers, results, and short-term first. The third scenario needs to deliver against hard KPIs, for sure, but probably a CMO may have the muscles to see beyond the here and now and imagine a different future, or at least the budget and people to do the short and long of it. We could call them Chief Total Marketing Officer. Maybe.

We are in flux. The world is ever changing, and nothing will be 100% perfect, once and for all. We hope this book helps, thanks to its theoretical concepts and real-life stories, current and futuristic, about the better world that we can and will build together. Thirty years ago, or so, Marketing was about serving fans. What if technology allowed us to learn from them, as we deliver our goods and services? What if all stakeholders could serve each other, enabled by data and technology, while zeroing out unnecessary burdens to the planet? Marketing is about vision. What if we could see better, if data were shared and data sources compensated fairly to keep feeding relevant information, at the right time and the right place? This requires us to be connected and, above all, to have a shared goal. Some will join for the money, some for the integration into a broader network. It doesn't matter. As said at the beginning of the book, this is a journey towards 2030, more or less. It's a bumpy road. It requires investment and a culture of change. Our goal was to draw a different future, or to serve as an appetizer of how the world could look like, if data were free to flow, and tech could help all humans to make sense of it.

Will we have that chance? We believe so. We believe, because we are human.

The Total Marketing Manifesto

Mara Cassinari

Frank Pagano

We believe in tech.

We believe that making sense of data can unlock value, while serving fans, employees and suppliers.

We believe that connecting and identifying digitally every individual on the planet will have more benefits than costs.

We believe in exponential technologies, like AI and blockchain, guided by the human desire to radically simplify the old and imagine the new.

We believe marketing should leverage tech to consume less of the earth, and rally everyone around a collaborative and open marketplace.

We believe the public arena, from health to education, from finance to energy, could turn into a profit, innovation and talent maker.

We believe in business, when co-created by suppliers, employees, and brand lovers out there, to craft products and services that inspire and delight.

We believe in success, shared across the food chain and compensated fairly, proportionally to everyone's willingness to dance.

We believe we can upgrade capitalism, and that marketing can change it all.

It's called Total Marketing for a reason.

We believe, because we are human.

Epilogue: Interview with Professor Daron Acemoglu[1]

Frank Pagano

Exponential technologies will change our world for good. This is our opinion, as tech optimists.

Now, it's always good to have a sanity check, or at least to have a listen to the contrarian view. We reached out to Daron Acemoglu, who is an Institute Professor of Economics at the Massachusetts Institute of Technology (MIT), a best-selling author, a world-know speaker, and the recipient of several prestigious prizes, among which the John Bates Clark Medal in 2005, given every two years to the best economist in the United States under the age of 40, by the American Economic Association. His resume is impressive, and Acemoglu is today one of the most quoted economists on the planet.

This is the exchange with the *Maestro*[2].

What exponential technologies will change our world, in your opinion, by 2030 - between Blockchain, AI, Spatial Computing, and Quantum?

Difficult to say. All of these are highly hyped. Which technologies will flourish and find impactful applications remains to be seen. I don't believe that blockchain has the potential to have pervasive effects except in a few narrow applications. AI is a different story. Even though much of what is written and said about AI is an exaggeration, there is no doubt that AI is advancing rapidly, and it is being rolled out in many sectors. Just on that basis, I expect it will impact many fields of the real economy, including social media, communication, and human resource management. Whether it can penetrate other activities, such as finance, law, education, and healthcare, remains to be seen. More importantly, even if it does become widely used in industries such as education and healthcare, there is a big difference between good use and bad use. For example, rolling out ChatGPT (by OpenAI) to millions of students and encouraging them to learn from the chatbot rather than their teachers is easy. Making sure that they learn the right material and learn effectively is much harder.

---

[1] Professor of Economics at the Massachusetts Institute of Technology (MIT) and recipient of the 2024 Nobel Prize in Economics.

[2] Written interview with Frank Pagano. 08/13/2024. Zurich.

AI is the land of the plausible, but not of the profitable. What is the business model to make AI financially healthy?

I would say it differently. Right now, the only place where AI can be used profitably is in social media and search-type activities, and even in this case, profits may come from manipulative uses (deep fakes, extensive information gathering, copyright violations, etc.) The key question is whether we can find a socially beneficial direction for AI, where it provides better information to humans, so that they can make better decisions and become capable of performing more sophisticated tasks. This is unclear, and unfortunately, it is not the area where industry has much interest.

I don't see the tech and cultural transformation of society and economy happening without a revision of our property rights. I need to own my medical records or digital agency, and get compensated for it, if AI or other tech stacks are going to use that (my) data to learn and serve society at large with better products and services. Do you see this happening? Can Meta, Alphabet, or Microsoft, for example, accept the fact that they will need to pay more stakeholders than they do today? Is that an illusion?

Absolutely. Data is a crucial input for AI, and right now, there is neither a market for data nor property rights on data, nor incentives for people to create high-quality data. This is both unfair (people's data is being stolen) and unproductive (AI models are being trained on low-quality data, contributing to the hallucinations and other problems of the available models). The solution must involve data markets and property rights on data. But it's complicated because individual property rights won't work. Billions of people produce valuable data, but transacting with billions of people would be prohibitively costly. More majorly, lots of people produce highly substitutable data (everybody can recognize a cat, so platforms can play one set of users against another to drive down the price of data). So, we need a new infrastructure for data markets with collective data ownership, for example, in the same way that the Writers Guild of America plays the role of an intermediary protecting the rights of creative artists and inducing a type of collective ownership.

Do you think the financial and banking system will accept at some point crypto, or even just bitcoin? What's your take on the future of the financial system, which should be open for all, and where financial fees should become a commodity, namely equal to zero?

I hope not. Right now, cryptocurrencies are valuable for three simple reasons: They permit illicit activities; there is some premium because if one of them becomes widely accepted, the company in charge of it would become fabulously wealthy; and there is a bubble component to many cryptocurrencies, with gullible investors sometimes being encouraged to pay excessive valuations for some currencies. None of those sources of valuation is socially beneficial. My view is that cryptocurrencies could be useful in some very narrow circumstances, but they should be very heavily regulated.

Do you think sustainability has had bad marketing so far? Shouldn't we chat about a total tech and marketing transformation of the world, where the world is run more efficiently? Should sustainability advocates look at tech as the only way to make this world less resource-intensive and less biased, and stop talking about ESG as a separate item on our to-do list?

ESG is a mishmash of many different things, very badly specified. Right now, it just empowers managers to do as they wish. Investors caring about the social good must be an important component of the market economy in the twenty-first century. For example, I believe that pressure from investors against fossil fuel companies could be quite effective. But this requires a very clear set of guidelines with measurable metrics. In the case of carbon emissions, we can do that. So, my preference would be to abandon ESG and to focus on carbon, and perhaps some other important issues, such as labor practices (for example, whether companies are creating highly unsafe environments for workers or putting coercive pressure on their employees).

The EU AI Act[3] seems to be the only regulation with some substance globally. Are we looking at a world where the rights of individuals will be sacrificed in the name of progress, if we look at the US and China? Who sets guidelines on AI?

Yes, absolutely, that's the real danger, and China is unlikely to play a leadership role here. The Chinese government is the biggest collector of data. The Chinese Communist Party is unlikely to be interested in protecting individual rights, and the evolution of the tech industry in China over the last two decades has created a culture in which intrusive data collection and surveillance have been normalized. The US regulators are still highly beholden to the whims and wishes of the tech industry. So far, leadership for reining in abusive practices in AI and the tech industry more generally must come from Europe. This is not sustainable if Europe itself doesn't become a big player in the AI field, and it doesn't seem like this is going to be easy. The hope is that the US political pendulum will swing in favor of more robust regulation and less influence of tech companies on policy, and in the meantime, Europe will start becoming an innovator, not just a regulator, of AI.

---

[3] For more information, check the EU Parliament website. For example, see: https://www.europarl.europa.eu/topics/en/article/20230601STO93804/eu-ai-act-first-regulation-on-artificial-intelligence.

Are you optimistic or pessimistic about the future of the world?

Neither. It's possible to use AI in a pro-worker way. It's possible to use AI to support democracy and better communication. It's possible to use AI consistently with individual rights, privacy and individual autonomy. But no, we are not heading in that direction. So if I believe that there will be no major redirection of technology and no major change in institutions in the United States and elsewhere, I would be very pessimistic. But I am clinging to the hope that it is possible for us to do a course correction, rein in the tech giants and start investing in AI that is good for people (and, in the process, also abandon crazy dreams about artificial general intelligence and disabuse ourselves of our continued trust in the tech giants.)

The Authors' Final Remarks

Mara Cassinari

Frank Pagano

This book is made of the same pragmatism as Professor Acemoglu's answers. We are not there yet. There is a lot to do if we want exponential technologies to serve the global community, instead of the very few, as has been the case for the web2 movement, incarnated by social media and big tech.

The potential is there, and the many use cases described here are testament to what our intellectual power and technology can do together. What we need are guidelines, standards, and internationally recognized property rights for our digital agency, so that we can make the future world taste like tech and humanity. What we also need is the awareness that the marketing job is never done. The world, made of consumers, employees and suppliers, will ask us, as managers and companies, to evolve with it. Only a continuous flow of data across the entire network will secure longevity for our enterprise and, especially, for the communities around our brands. Total Marketing is dynamic and ever evolving. The mitigation of any risk associated with that evolution is in the wise use of exponential technologies. What's a wise decision when we handle tech?

The first question of any C Room, as mentioned in our Chapter 2, is: "How do we do it, profitably and pragmatically?" and we have demonstrated that tech can be a key enabler. The last question that we want to leave with the reader is: "Do we want a more human world?" and tech is not enough for that answer. The world will be filled with immense power and capabilities in the next five years, almost like the vital fuel for a fast and long trip to a different future. We are asking the fan, the manager and the supplier of the future, empowered by the weapons of their Total Marketing: "Where are we going?" This is a profoundly human question. This is what Marketers must focus on. It's their only occupation, now that they are freed from the rest of their tasks.

Afterword – 1

Giuseppe Stigliano[1]

Purpose, People, Planet, therefore Profit. This is the title of one of the chapters in the latest book I co-authored with Philip Kotler[2]. In that chapter, we argue, much like the authors of this book, that successful companies of the future must act decisively as social agents. They will need to be clear about what they stand for, take a stance on societal priorities, and actively work to create social value.

As Marco Di Dio Roccazzella suggested in the Foreword, technology will finally allow organizations to discover the "holy grail" of marketing—the right product or content, to the right person, at the right time. This shift will likely fulfill the vision of marketing's pioneers, who aimed to "make things people want" rather than merely "make people want things." However, achieving this will require tremendous attention to the way customer data is managed.

Gone are the days when people would passively accept the notion: "If it's not clear what the product is, it means that 'you' are the product." In the future, consumers will expect a fair value exchange between their data and the benefits they receive in return. As the authors suggest, successful companies will build trust by transparently informing customers and stakeholders about data usage, advocating ethical data practices, and fostering a mutually beneficial relationship. This concept includes data value-sharing, where businesses give back some of the value generated from data to consumers, thereby strengthening trust through ethical engagement.

At the heart of Total Marketing lies the belief that experiences should not exist in silos. Creating value for the market and customers alone will no longer suffice to define a successful business. A purposeful organization must consistently "walk the talk" across all touchpoints, offering a holistic, interconnected experience across both customer and employee interactions. This concept also embraces the idea of seamless interactions across devices— mobile, web, wearables, and augmented reality. Multi-experience aims to deliver consistent, adaptive experiences, ensuring a cohesive journey for users, regardless of how or where they engage with the brand.

---

[1] President at Spring Studio, Author, Speaker, University Professor.

[2] G. Stigliano, P. Kotler, *Redefining Retail. 10 Guiding Principles For a Post-Digital World*, Wiley, 2024.

As we conclude our exploration of Total Marketing, it's clear that the path forward for businesses is not merely strategic evolution but a fundamental transformation. In a world where technology permeates every interaction, the boundaries between customer, employee, and brand experiences dissolve, creating a seamless, interconnected ecosystem. This book aims not only to define what Total Marketing is but also to challenge traditional approaches, urging us to see beyond isolated transactions and instead embrace a holistic, human-centered vision.

Customer Experience, Employee Experience, User Experience, and Multiexperience must converge to build a foundation that is more responsive, adaptable, and attuned to the complexities of today's market. Companies that thrive will not just adapt technology but wield it with purpose. Artificial intelligence, blockchain, and other exponential technologies offer remarkable efficiencies and personalization capabilities, yet they also demand a new level of responsibility. As we use data to enhance experiences, we must handle it with respect and transparency, recognizing that trust is now the currency of success.

The journey of Total Marketing is not just a strategy for organizational efficiency or customer loyalty; it's a step toward creating a more inclusive, equitable business environment where every stakeholder, from consumers to suppliers to employees, shares in the value generated. It calls for a shift from transactional relationships to meaningful, lasting connections. In closing, this book is a call to action for business leaders, marketers, and innovators alike. Embracing Total Marketing is about more than staying competitive; it's about setting the standards for a future where business thrives in harmony with people and planet. The question now is not just whether we can implement these changes but whether we are willing to. As we look to the future, may we carry forward the insights gained here to build companies that are resilient, responsive, and, above all, deeply human.

Afterword – 2

Massimo Morini[1]

This book is an incredible source of new ideas, case studies, explanations, and examples about the application of disruptive technologies across multiple markets. It can serve as a handbook for effective and revolutionary marketing strategies. Alternatively, as it was for me, not being a marketing person, it offers a thought-provoking reflection on how our relationship with the "products" we buy is transforming and will continue to evolve soon.

If traditional marketing, with its "4 Ps" (Promotion, Place, Price, Product), was rooted in the perspective of the "Producers," this new approach to marketing takes the viewpoint of the Clients rather than the Producers. I see four "Cs" replacing the Ps: *Choice* rather than Promotion; *Connection* rather than Place; *Certainty* (or if you prefer *Certification*) as the foundation for fair Pricing; the Product will become the *Center* of a network of services, interests, and values, directly chosen and activated by consumers, with benefits reverberating to all stakeholders.

From this new perspective, the book highlights several important points, which are relevant to my own field of business and research: technology and its impact on the economy.

First, the book demonstrates how AI should be applied: as an extension and empowerment of human rights, or choices, and not as a superior replacement for them.

Second, and maybe more importantly, it reminds us that this transformation cannot occur without the support of other technologies, specifically designed to shift power from big tech, banks, and large corporations to individuals, and able to create, transfer, and monetize value without the need for intermediaries. This shift is already happening with blockchain-native products, where tokens are created, sold, bought, resold, or swapped by participants in the economy, eliminating traditional intermediation. The extension of this concept also to physical and digital products, which may not be born as blockchain-native, thanks also to AI, represents one of the most significant revolutions of the near future. If embraced by companies and entrepreneurs, this shift can unlock new value and save costs for all sides of any market.

---

[1] Massimo Morini is a Professor at Bocconi University, Milan Politecnico and USI (Università della Svizzera Italiana).

Decentralized markets reduce the issues related to replacements, upgrades, and warranties, benefiting both companies and consumers. They enable immediate rewards for customer actions that enhance company value, a concept that has been a dream since the birth of cryptocurrencies, but that was initially infeasible due to high costs and transaction fees. In recent years, projects like Algorand and Cardano[2], as well as Layer-2 solutions on Ethereum, have enabled thousands of transactions per second at minimal costs, making this vision a reality. Many projects are mentioned in the book. Blockchain is still improving, which means that early adopters and entrepreneurs still have opportunities to become first movers.

Decentralized platforms also bring transparency, offering certification and validation for production and business processes that were previously obscure and not always aligned with clients' interests. This can also be applied to AI-related processes. Encryption, smart contracts, and lesser-known technologies like hashing and zero-knowledge proof (ZKP,)[3] can make AI processes verifiable from data sources to algorithms, while respecting privacy and returning ultimate control to end users. At the pace of recent innovation, we are nearing a world where AI and blockchain will work together to expand our capabilities without sacrificing our freedom and awareness. An ultimate dream, just a few steps ahead of our current capabilities.

What is already achievable, and the roadmap for the most immediate and likely business opportunities, can be found, with plenty of clear and simple examples, in this book by Frank Pagano and Mara Cassinari, dedicated to a new world, shaped by Total Marketing.

---

[2] Massimo Morini has been part of the founding group of Algorand and is an advisor at Cardano, both Layer 1 and first-generation blockchains. Ethereum is also a Layer 1 blockchain, and probably the most used and popular one, after Bitcoin. Mr. Morini is one of the world's most authoritative experts in the field of blockchain, especially when applied to Finance. For more information, see: www.algorand.co and www.cardano foundation.org.

[3] The case of the Mina Foundation, reported in Chapter 2, shows the utility of ZKP.

Index

www.ingramcontent.com/pod-product-compliance
Lightning Source LLC
Chambersburg PA
CBHW050516280326
41932CB00014B/2339